D1478983

1,001 Ways to Reuse
Your Stuff So You . . .

# DON'T
# THROW
# THAT
# AWAY!

Jeff Yeager

# Also by Jeff Yeager:

*The Cheapskate Next Door*

*The Ultimate Cheapskate's Road Map to True Riches*

*How to Retire the Cheapskate Way*

To my grandparents, Ellen and Clyde Yeager and Irma and Kenneth "Tex" Cooper,  and to everyone who, like them, lived through the Great Depression.

The motto of that Greatest Generation was "Use it up, wear it out, make it do, or do without." May we learn from that and always remember them.

# Table of Contents

# Don't Throw That Away!

# Chapter 1
## Reduce—Reuse, Reuse, Reuse, and Reuse Again—*Then* Recycle

I don't know when "repurposing"—finding ways to reuse things that might otherwise be thrown away—became a word.

And depending on which dictionary you believe, it may still not be a real word. This, despite the fact that today you can't attend any gathering from a cocktail party to a PTA meeting without words like "repurposing," "renewable," "sustainability," and "recyclable" cropping up in the conversation.

When you think about it, "repurposing"—also known as "upcycling"—should have been one of the first words ever invented. After all, we've been doing it since Clovis Man realized that the tusk of the mammoth he just slayed would make a dandy weapon with which to bludgeon more mammoths. Or, depending on your historical and religious perspectives, ever since Adam and Eve discovered there's more than one use for the modest **fig leaf**. (FYI, they're also great for wrapping fish in and then grilling).

Heck, I'm thinking that maybe even those big stone slabs at Stonehenge were actually leftover granite countertops from some Druid's prehistoric kitchen remodeling project. "Honey, go out in the yard and stand those twenty-ton stone fragments up on end. I think they'll look a lot better than the neighbor's lawn jockeys carved out of mammoths' tusks, don't you?"

But it's only been recently—thanks in part to the economic belt tightening prompted by the recession and the burgeoning green movement—that we've begun to rediscover something that those souls who lived through the Great Depression—and those who lived before—came to know so well: There are all kinds of practical, money-saving ways to reuse stuff that our generation has come to simply throw away.

That's what this book is about. It's entirely devoted to the second element of the old environmentalist's mantra: Reduce, *Reuse*, Recycle.

In the pages ahead you'll find hundreds of ways to repurpose all sorts of would-be throwaway items, from everyday practical tips to truly bizarre examples of *über repurposing*. As the Ultimate Cheapskate, I'll be sharing some of my own favorite repurposing tips and tricks with you, as well as tons of others supplied by my Miser Advisers, a worldwide network of fellow frugal folks who volunteer as my bargain-basement brain trust. I can guarantee that you'll save both a lot of money and the earth's resources if you adopt even a fraction of the ideas offered in this book. And I promise you'll have fun and be introduced to some colorful gurus-of-re-purposing along the way. (Did that lady in Michigan really make a mural out of **dryer lint**, and then sell it for $12,000?)

As you can see from the table of contents, chapters in the book are devoted to general topics or themes (e.g., repurposing items in the bathroom, repurposing items for the holidays, etc.) as opposed to specific throwaway items. But the index at the back of the book is organized by individual items that can be repurposed. So, if you're wondering what you can do with that worn-out pair of pantyhose, that out-of-date phone book, or the milk that just went sour, consult the index to find references to those items in various chapters throughout the book.

But whatever you do, *Don't Throw That Away!*

## Why Bother?

Everybody seems to have a notoriously frugal, rather eccentric, great-aunt Maggie. You know, the one who saves and reuses her **Ziploc baggies** until their zip is entirely zapped.

When you were a kid, she wrapped your birthday presents in the **Sunday comic**. The secondhand knapsack she gave you for high school graduation—the one you still use whenever you travel—was even more cleverly wrapped in a slightly outdated **map** of the world that the local library was going to throw away. And family legend has it that Great-Aunt Maggie has been using and reusing the same sheet of **aluminum foil** since the Johnson administration (we're talking Andrew Johnson, not LBJ).

Maybe you even get an occasional chuckle about your great-aunt Maggie and her penny-pinching practices.

Having spent most of my life living what I call the "cheapskate lifestyle" and hanging out with more baggle-saving great-aunts and great-uncles than you can imagine, I'd venture to say that you might not chuckle if you scratch beneath the surface and take a closer look at their lives. I'd guess that your great-aunt Maggie, despite her aluminum foil fetish, probably has fewer money worries than most people you know. She's probably managed to live debt-free for most her life. And even though everyone rolls their eyes when she insists on taking home every scrap of leftovers from the family reunion rather than throw anything away, she may very well be the person who everyone in the family knows they can turn to if they're in need of some financial help.

By all accounts, Verna Oller of Long Beach, Washington, was just such a great aunt. To save money, she shopped exclusively at thrift stores, cut her own hair, and repurposed the **zippers** from worn-out clothing to replace the shoelaces in her work boots rather than buy new. Having worked most of her life as a lowly paid fish cleaner, when Oller died in 2010 at the age of ninety-eight, she left a surprise fortune of $4.5 million to build a swimming pool in her community and fund local scholarships and grants. I'll bet the people in her community aren't chuckling about Verna and her frugal ways any longer.

Now, I'm not claiming that weaving your own throw rugs out of **bread wrappers** will make you rich (although they are pretty, and making them can be fun—see Chapter 6). Like a lot of thrifty folks, Verna Oller was a savvy investor as well as a disciplined saver; that was the double-barreled key to her financial good fortunes. But I will bet that if you start incorporating a few simple acts of frugality into your own life—like saving and reusing that **aluminum foil**—you'll be surprised how little savings can really add up.

Far more important, these tiny acts of savings are likely to foster in you a broader *ethic of thrift* that might very well change your life—and your relationship with money—forever. You may discover, as I did in my own life, that when you pinch the pennies, the dollars usually pinch themselves. When you challenge yourself to waste less by repurposing items you previously considered disposable, I'll wager that your perspective on life and money will slowly start to change, and change for the best.

You'll probably start to think twice about buying things you don't really need. You're likely to start pausing before whipping out your credit card to pay for something, particularly if you know that when the bill for that item comes in the mail, you won't be able to fully pay it. You might also realize that you can now afford to set aside at least a little money for a rainy day, when before it seemed impossible . . . because every day it was raining.

Yes, all that can start with something as simple as reusing your baggies. That's what Great-Aunt Maggie *really* has to teach you.

## Shocking Eco Facts

But repurposing would-be throwaway stuff isn't just about saving you money. It's also about helping to save the planet. Throughout this book, we'll be pausing from time to time to look at some "Shocking Eco Facts." That's "eco" as in both "ecological" and "economical," the true costs associated with the throwaway society we live in. Here are some examples of such fascinating factoids:

- According to the Natural Resources Defense Council (NRDC.org), the U.S. airline industry throws away enough **aluminum cans** from their in-flight beverage services every year to build fifty-eight new 747 aircrafts. The industry says it's been working to improve its on-board recycling efforts. But as long as they're nickel-and-diming passengers for everything from checked bags to bags of nuts, shouldn't they at least be doing their part to help the environment and save money by building their planes out of Coke cans instead of throwing them away? Heck, they should talk to Wayne Mathis of Helena, Montana; he's been building prototypes of flying beer and soda cans at B.C. Air Originals—B.C. as in Beverage Cans—since 1984 (bcair.com).

- The average American generates about 4.5 pounds of solid waste every day, says the U.S. Environmental Protection Agency (EPA.gov). Of that, approximately 24.3 percent is recycled, 8.9 percent is composted (including yard waste), and 66.8 percent is sent to a landfill or incinerated. The good news is that Americans are recycling more waste than in the past. The bad news is that Americans are also generating more waste than in the past, up from only about 2.68 pounds per person per day in the 1960s. In total (net of what was recycled), we threw away 82.5 million tons of solid waste in 1960, and 161 million tons in 2009, despite an almost fifteenfold increase in the tonnage being recycled. One step forward, two steps back. It's also worth noting that the United States makes up only 4 percent of the world's population but is the number one producer of garbage. It's good to still be number one in something, I guess.

- We see them every day: **Plastic shopping bags** strewn everywhere, the new blight on America the Beautiful. As consumers, we spend about $4 billion a year on those flimsy, ugly bags, the cost built into the products we buy. Only about 5 percent of them ever get recycled; little wonder, since it costs about $4,000 to process and recycle one ton of plastic bags (we use about four MILLION tons annually), the by-product of which can then be sold on the commodities market for around $40. So, most of them end up in the landfill, where they take roughly five hundred years to decompose. Although with so many plastic bags literally floating around everywhere you look, increasingly they're being consumed by marine and land animals, including domestic livestock, and they are entering the human food chain. One of my Miser Advisers, Antonia Bookbinder, decided to make a statement—a symbolic as well as a fashionable one—against plastic shopping bags by crocheting a reusable shopping bag out of dozens of the disposable variety. Plus carrying your own reusable bags to the supermarket will get you a discount at many stores.

- What's staggering about how much stuff we throw away or waste isn't just the sheer volume of it, but the amount of time creative journalists and environmentalists spend developing comparisons between those wasted resources and what they represent. Some of my favorites:
  * Americans throw away enough **office paper** each year to build a wall of paper twelve feet high from New York to Los Angeles (maybe the folks who support the building of a wall along the U.S./Mexican border should look into that). * Recycling one **aluminum can** saves enough energy to operate a TV for three

hours (a great point to remember next time my wife gets on my case for drinking beer while watching TV). * In a lifetime, the average American will throw away six hundred times his or her body weight in solid waste (another good reason to watch your weight).

## Start with a Trash Can Autopsy

I love talking trash. I also love listening to trash. I love listening to what the contents of a trash can has to say about the people who threw that stuff away and how they live.

Archaeologists will tell you that a society's garbage heap often reveals more about people and their culture than any other artifacts they leave behind. For example, archaeologists excavating Monte Testaccio—an ancient Roman dumping ground one mile in circumference and smack-dab in the midst of modern-day Rome's trendiest neighborhood—are revealing the role olive oil played in the lives and finances of early Romans through the nearly twenty-five million shipping amphorae dumped there. Apparently ancient Romans loved their olive oil as much as we love our bottled water, and they left a similar trail of trash evidence to prove it.

Before we dive into ways to repurpose things you're probably throwing away every day, first take a few minutes to dive into your garbage can and recycling bin by doing a Trash Can Autopsy. That's right: Roll up your sleeves, put on some rubber gloves, and pick through a week's worth of your family's refuse.

I'll bet that if you take the time to do it and listen to what your trash is trying to tell you about how you're throwing away your money, you'll find some simple ways to save hundreds—maybe even thousands—of dollars per year.

Here are some things to be on the lookout for when performing your Trash Can Autopsy.

**Packaging:** Lots and lots of **packaging** in your trash is a sure sign that you need a smart-shopping intervention. All that packaging costs money, which you're paying for in the end. Try buying in bulk, shopping at food co-ops, and avoiding elaborately packaged products whenever possible—it's usually much cheaper and saves natural resources. While larger containers are typically a better value than smaller sizes, that isn't always the case, so be sure to check the "per unit price" label on the store shelf when comparing items just to be certain.

**Food Waste:** According to the USDA (USDA.gov), nearly 25 percent of all food sold in America ends up in the garbage can. So if you're a typical American family, you could reduce your grocery bill by a quarter simply by being smarter about portion control and food storage. Of course there are plenty of ways to creatively repurpose **leftover food** items—even after they're past their prime—as you'll see in Chapter 4.

**Dryer Lint:** Are you throwing away lots of **dryer lint**? Consider this: Dryer lint represents the life of your expensive clothing being beaten and cooked out of them by an electric dryer. The process of washing and drying clothing is typically harder on fabric than everyday wear and tear. By drying clothing on an old-fashioned clothesline, your duds will last as much as 50 percent longer and you'll save about $200 per year on electricity and appliance costs as well.

**Lightbulbs:** For every five to ten burned-out incandescent **lightbulbs** that you pitch in the trash can, a single long-lasting "compact florescent lamp" or "CFL"—those crazy corkscrew lightbulbs—could still be burning bright and using about 75 percent less electricity. Although CFLs cost a bit more than incandescent bulbs, you'll have a *net savings* of about $10+ per year for every incandescent bulb you replace with a CFL.

**Fruit and Vegetable Scraps:** You're throwing away valuable vitamins, fiber, and other nutrients you've already paid for if you have things like **apple, cucumber, and potato peels** in your trash. The skins of fruits and veggies often contain more nutrients than the flesh, and they should be eaten or at least used in soup stock whenever possible (after thoroughly washing, of course). What you don't eat, I'm sure your compost pile will enjoy (see Chapter 8), and there are a multitude of ways to repurpose specific types of fruit and veggie skins, particularly for cosmetic and medicinal purposes (see Chapter 3).

**Magazines and Newspapers:** Sure they can be recycled and/or repurposed in a number of ways, but why not save both money and trees by canceling your subscriptions and reading them online or borrowing them from the library instead?

**Fast-Food and Carryout Containers:** Are you finding a lot of pizza boxes and burger bags in your trash? The U.S. Census Bureau (Census.gov) reports that the typical American family now spends nearly 45 percent of its food budget on meals prepared outside the home. Try at least cutting back on restaurant and carryout meals by preparing more meals at home and you'll save as much as 80 percent compared to the restaurant price. Cook batch recipes and freeze the leftovers to make the fastest food of all—a dish that's already waiting for you at home.

**Plastic Water Bottles:** Did you know that if you drink only bottled water, you'll spend more than $1,000 annually to get your recommended daily amount of $H_2O$, as opposed to about 49 cents for a year's supply of just-as-healthy tap water? Talk about getting soaked! **Plastic water bottles** are really hard on the environment, too; 1.5 million barrels of oil are used every year to produce plastic water bottles for the U.S. market. Ironically, it also takes about three liters of water to manufacture a one-liter water bottle!

**Household Cleaning Products:** We've gone absolutely daffy over household cleaning products. There's now a different—and expensive—cleaning product for every room and item in the house. You probably have a spending problem if you see empty bottles from a plethora of household cleansers in your trash. Most items in the home can be cleaned with simple household supplies like baking soda, vinegar, and a multitude of repurposed items as you'll see shortly. Cleaning with these common household items can save you a bucketful of money, and they're often even more eco-friendly than expensive "green" cleaning products you buy in the store.

**Brand Names:** Does your trash look like the logo lineup from the commercials at Super Bowl halftime? If so, you're probably wasting money on expensive brand-name products when many generic items are often just as good—or even better. Generic and store brands generally cost 20 to 50 percent less than comparable brand-name products. At least give generic equivalents a try, starting with those products you buy most frequently.

**Lawn Clippings: Grass clippings** and other organic material from the yard should always be returned to nature via the compost pile rather than entombed in a plastic bag and sent to the landfill for the better part of eternity. And consider reducing the size of your lawn by planting a low-maintenance ground cover or covering part of it with mulch. Lawns are hard on both our wallets and the environment, with all the water, pesticides, and fertilizer they require.

**Things You Don't Know What to Do With:** Next time you go to throw away something you no longer want, ask yourself if someone else could use it. Sell unwanted items at a yard sale or online to make a little extra cash, or give them away for free via websites like freecycle.org or craigslist.com. And donating items to a thrift store or other charity (see Chapter 8) usually gives you a tax deduction and helps those in need. It's a real win-win!

Now that you've listened to what your trash is trying to tell you about how you're wasting money, let's get creative and look at some ways—1,001 ways, in fact—to repurpose those things you're still throwing away.

## Repurposing: A Proud Family Tradition

A friend of mine once said about me, "Jeff's never met a piece of **scrap lumber** he didn't love." That's true—and flattering—because I come from a long line of creative repurposers. Their thrift-craft hardened by the Great Depression, both sets of my grandparents had extraordinary skills for stretching resources by inventing new ways to use and reuse whatever items they had on hand.

My grandpa Tex Cooper taught me how to render **catfish fat** into an oil he'd apply to any and all leather items he owned, particularly his prized cowboy boots. It kept the leather soft and made it last longer, he insisted. The downside: Tex was constantly accompanied by an entourage of neighborhood cats and dogs when he walked down the street.

My grandma Cooper, Irma, was a David Copperfield in the kitchen, able to magically produce scrumptious meals out of a seemingly bare kitchen cupboard. No morsel of anything was ever thrown away. Rather, it would be reincarnated—even tastier than before—in another dish a few days later.

And my other grandfather, Clyde Yeager, was one of the great diluters of his time. He'd stretch milk, ketchup, and all manner of food products by adding water, and use inexpensive linseed oil to dilute most everything else. He taught me a magical secret—the Yeager family alchemy—of the "drippins jar" (see Chapter 4). By the time Clyde threw out a **jar or other container**—*if* he threw it out, that is—it'd be "cleaner than a frog's armpit," as he liked to say.

But it was my grandma Yeager, Ellen, who actually moved beyond repurposing as a utilitarian practice. For Grandma Yeager, it eventually became pure sport.

She had a passion for recycling would-be throwaways into clever craft items, most of which served no earthly purpose, other than the joy she received from creating them. **Coffee cans** were ensconced in poodle-shaped crocheted covers to conceal spare rolls of toilet paper in the bathroom. **Plastic soda bottles** were transformed into wind-catching pinwheels and impaled on stakes in the backyard. An empty **bleach bottle** was painted hot pink to look like a happy piggy and positioned atop the fridge, emblazoned with the words, "Go ahead and open it! You'll look just like me!"

At Christmastime, Ellen's craftiness was in full zenith. She fashioned wreaths from folded **IBM computer "punch cards,"** a Midwestern take on origami, I suppose. Eight tiny reindeer were actually **toilet paper tubes** with pipe cleaner legs and antlers and **half shells of walnuts** for heads (who knew?). And—my personal favorite—a festive yuletide "disco ball" hung in the doorway, made of glitter-covered **specimen cups** repurposed from Grandpa Yeager's urological visits and studded with plastic holly leaves and berries.

I somehow could never bring myself to kiss my bride-to-be under that mock mistletoe, despite all the repurposing love I knew that Grandma had put into making it.

# Chapter 2
## Home Building, Remodeling, and Decorating

**Answer:** *We use it to insulate the inside of our windows in the winter, mostly in rooms we don't use that much or odd-shaped windows. You just cut it to the right size, spray the glass with water (from inside the house), and press it "bubble side" first onto the wet windowpane. It sticks like magic, and comes off clean, just by pulling. It really cut down on our heating bill, and it was free!*
Bob M. (Joplin, Missouri)

**Question**: *What can you do with leftover **"bubble wrap"**?* (Bob also suggests checking with furniture stores—and places that sell canoes!—which often have large quantities of bubble wrap they're happy to give away.)

"How would you describe the style of your ah . . . ah . . . *house*, Jeff?" a visitor once asked me.

"Well, I haven't really thought about it like that. You know, a 'style' and all," I said, looking as if for the first time at the ramshackle-come-eclectic-come-sometimes-beautiful warren of buildings we've happily called home for the past twenty-five years. Finally I said, "I guess, maybe, 'Early Branch Davidian Compound'?"

Living in—and endlessly remodeling—a house made in part from reclaimed and recycled materials myself, I was both fascinated and comforted to learn about the important work of Texas homebuilder Dan Phillips.

I was *fascinated* because Phillips builds attractive, affordable (some costing as little as $10,000), energy-efficient homes for low-income families, largely out of materials that would otherwise end up as trash. He estimates that 70 to 80 percent of the building materials he uses are recycled or reclaimed—as in saved from the landfill—or creatively repurposed, like the hollowed-out **eggshells** and **nutshells** he fills with resin to use as the type of architectural details traditional builders pay a premium for in the form of milled hardwood embellishments.

And I was *comforted* to learn of Phillips's work and have a chance to interview him because if the House of Yeager is "unique," it ain't nothing compared to some of the homes Dan and his firm Phoenix Commotion build (phoenixcommotion.com).

For example, there's the "Bone House," one of several unusual homes Dan has built in Huntsville, Texas, outside of Houston. No, it's not a home he built for Mr. and Mrs. Bone. It's a house constructed in part out of actual **animal bones** ("Mostly cattle bones," he told me when I was naive enough to ask. "This is Texas, you know?"), including both functional and decorative applications. On the more practical side, bones are used as door handles and even in the construction of a staircase, while they're also incorporated in decorative wall hangings and furnishings both inside and outside the home.

Then there's the "License Plate House," featuring a roof constructed of over five thousand **license plates** people returned to the tax office for new ones. Phillips asked the good folks at the tax office to save them for him, and the result is a heavy-duty—and traffic-stopping—roof that he estimates will last "at least 75 years."

And that's only the tip of Dan Phillips's creative talents when it comes to building one-of-a-kind structures out of unusual and oftentimes reclaimed materials. There's the "Budweiser House" (complete with beer taps substituted for traditional faucets in the bathroom), the ongoing "Butterfly Glass House," and the interior of a recycling education center Dan was commissioned to design and build for Waste Management of Houston, an international solid waste company. The company has to be pretty pleased with the materials budget for that project, since Dan constructed much of it—including a number of large murals—out of materials Waste Management would otherwise need to pay to dispose of.

In a speech Dan gave in 2010 as part of the TED speaking series, ted.com/talks/lang/eng/dan_phillips_ creative_houses_from_reclaimed_stuff.html, he hit the (repurposed) nail on the head when he talked about the *BIG Y*: as in "why so many usable building materials end up in landfills." Phillips says it all comes back to a building industry and culture that places a priority on "consistency," "patterns," and "premeditated models."

"If you have a wall of **windows**, and one pane is cracked . . . let's take it out, and throw it away so nobody can use it . . . because that's what you do with a cracked pane. Never mind that it doesn't affect our lives at all . . . it only rattles that expected unity of structural features." If you can't accept that type of inconsequential flaw and the way it interrupts the consistency of the pattern, Phillips suggests instead maybe you should take a hammer and crack all the other windows so they match rather than throw away the one cracked pane.

Dan Phillips: the Obi-Wan Kenobi of home-building creative repurposing.

## Shocking Eco Facts

Anyone interested in some *home leftovers*? There are plenty to go around. According to a study by the National Association of Home Builders (nahb.org), approximately eight thousand pounds of waste is generated from the construction of a new two-thousand-square-foot home. Most of that is in the form of wood, drywall, and cardboard. The EPA (EPA.gov) says that roughly 40 percent of all solid waste in landfills is construction-related material (new construction as well as remodels and demolitions, both residential and commercial projects). Ultimately the home buyer

/owner is paying for those leftovers, including more than $500 just to have the debris hauled away from the job site. Much of the waste could be avoided by builders being more exact when ordering materials, buying bulk materials rather than highly packaged products, and reusing more materials on the job site. While nearly 90 percent of construction site materials could be recycled, only about 20 percent actually is.

## The Reclaimed Home

Here are some ways reclaimed and repurposed items are incorporated into home construction and remodeling.

*Tired* **of the Same Old Type of House?**: Consider building a so-called earthship—a passive solar house made of natural and recycled materials, most notably a freeway's worth of old **car and truck tires**. The idea dates back to the 1970s—when a lot of people were experimenting with a lot of things—and an architect in New Mexico named Mike Reynolds who began experimenting with old car tires and their possible applications in home construction. He discovered that when tires are "rammed" (that's earthship-speak) full of ordinary dirt and stacked on top of one another (usually in a horseshoe-shaped design), they create nearly indestructible, naturally thermal insulated building walls that—because of the soil inside—are also highly fire resistant. Sometimes the tires are purposely left visible from outside or inside the house, although often the tires are concealed under adobe, plaster, or some other less *tiresome* and more attractive material. With more than two hundred million used tires being replaced every year in the United States—and recycling/ disposal being both costly and difficult—there's no shortage of raw materials available for earthship home construction. It's just a matter of getting things rolling, so to speak. Mike Reynolds's firm Earthship Biotecture (earthship.com) is a good place to start.

**Let There Be Light:** Simple "solar bottle lights" made out of **plastic soda bottles** are lighting up homes and other buildings in the Philippines and elsewhere. The lights, which only provide illumination during the day, are primarily installed in windowless buildings with steel roofs. That makes them perfect for my garage and toolshed. The bottles are filled with a mixture of water and a little chlorine bleach, and then mounted in a piece of metal flashing, which is inserted into a hole in the roof and properly sealed. The chlorine in the bleach helps to keep the water clear and better refract the sun's rays, creating 55 watts worth of light per bottle. Check out this video for how simple technology and a commonly thrown away item can dramatically improve people's lives: youtube.com/watch?v=kDL52lTri5c.

**Talk About Carpet Burn:** Forget about Occupy Wall Street. Why not Carpet Wall Street? According to the nonprofit environmental organization Green Seal (greenseal.org), more than five billion pounds of carpeting ends up in the landfill every year, enough to carpet an area larger than New York City. Before throwing away **old carpet**, consider salvaging any nicer portions (e.g., areas that have been protected by furniture or around the edges) to recarpet a smaller space, like a bathroom or closet, or your car or even car trunk. Cut pads of old carpet to fit under furniture and appliances to keep them from scraping hard-surfaced floors and make them easier to move. Or remodel your dog's and cat's houses with old carpet remnants. And if you have a cat, cover a log or length of wooden post with carpet remnants (attaching them with a staple gun), then secure to a base board with screws to make a cat scratching post.

**Flooring Ideas That Will Really Floor You:** As you might guess, when it comes to flooring, Dan Phillips isn't a big fan of carpeting and other traditional flooring materials. He suggests that if you have an existing home and you're looking for a way to incorporate some repurposed materials into it—both to save some money and resources and make your home truly special—the floors are a good place to start. Depending on the type of subfloor you have, the options vary, but some of Dan's favorite materials for flooring include: **scrap lumber** used in mosaic design ("Glue is a marvelous thing and allows the permutations of a wooden floor to be endless," he writes on his website); random pieces of scrap **tile** and pieces of **stone**—even gluing stones from your driveway to the floor; adobe or simply painting subfloors with textural patterns, stencils, or other designs. One of Dan's signature methods for repurposing materials to create unique and durable floors is, believe it or not, papier-mâché. Papier-mâché floors—which are protected under multiple layers of urethane—allow you to really get creative by repurposing all types of **scrap paper and cardboard**, including **paper bags**, **product labels**, **event posters**, **magazine features**, even **newspaper comics**. And the floor Dan once covered entirely in **wine corks** (supplied by wine connoisseurs from all across the country) may not be practical for everyone, but it's something to toast.

**Novel Room Dividers:** When you think about it, within the confines of the exterior and any other load-bearing walls, houses are really just empty shells. That presents unlimited opportunities to divide and re-divide (or not) the space with interior walls and other types of partitions, both permanent and temporary. In our own home remodeling projects, we've opted to keep much of the space as flexible as possible, including the installation of sliding "shoji screens"—commonly used in Asian architecture—to allow for spaces to be opened up or closed off as desired. We always loved the look and practicality of shoji screens, but not the price. When we eventually found some used at a Re-Store (see below) our design plans were decided for us. (We were told that they came from a local sushi restaurant that went out of business, and for the entire set of screens we paid only slightly more than we'd likely have spent for a couple of California rolls and the deluxe sushi platter at the same restaurant.) When it comes to room dividers, there are many alternatives to traditional drywall or wood-paneled walls. In earthship homes, interior non-load-bearing walls are often "tin can walls" (more earthship-speak), made of a honeycomb of repurposed **tin cans** joined with concrete and occasionally incorporating **glass bottles** to let through sunlight. In some cases, empty wine and other **glass bottles** are used to construct an entire "glass wall" simply by stacking them between upright support posts and fastening them together with a little glue. Other options include screening off portions of a room with temporary dividers or hanging curtains made from everything from **fabric remnants** to chains of old **CDs or DVDs**. And one of my Miser Advisers really had a *novel approach*: He made a partial room divider by stacking and gluing together hundreds of **old books** that his local library system was getting ready to send to the recycling plant.

**Now *That's* Aluminum Siding:** "I guess I just thought it was a good idea. And it's easier than painting," the late John Milkovisch is famously quoted as saying. John's words likely capture the interest of many homeowners, always looking for an easier alternative to painting the house. But John's solution—his "good idea"—has made him a legend to this day in his hometown of Houston, Texas. In 1968, when the retired upholsterer's house needed painting, he decided to opt for aluminum siding instead. Then John realized that maybe he could leverage one of his other passions in order to get all the aluminum siding he needed. "He just loved drinking his beer," his wife, Mary, said. And so it started. John began flattening his empty **beer cans** and fastening them to the sides of the house. By the time the house was fully clad in cans, John was enjoying his newfound hobby (and one can only assume the process of procuring the necessary raw materials as well) too much to just stop. He then began cutting beer cans and fashioning them into "garlands" and other accoutrements for the outside of the house. Among other things he discovered through his experimentation in the Beer Can Sciences was that the garlands sounded like beautiful wind chimes when the breeze blew, and they helped to lower the Milkovisches' heating bill considerably by sheltering the house. Another quote attributed to John Milkovisch, who died in 1988 at the age of seventy-five, resonates with many of us who are passionate about creative repurposing: "Some people say this is sculpture but I didn't go to no expensive school to get these crazy notions." Today the "Beer Can House" (beercanhouse.org) is maintained as a Houston landmark and is open to the public.

**ReStores for Real Deals:** Even if you're not into repurposing crazy materials like old car tires, wine corks, soda bottles, or crushed beer cans to use in building or remodeling your home, you can find all types of traditional building materials—both new and used—by visiting a "ReStore" (habitat.org/restores/) operated by the nonprofit organization Habitat for Humanity. They sell donated building materials including windows, doors, lumber, plumbing fixtures, paint, appliances, and just about anything else needed to build or decorate a home, inside and out. It's a chance to save money and the earth's resources, while supporting a good organization at the same time. And remember, they're always looking for donated materials, too.

## More Nifty-Thrifty Repurposing Tips for Home Remodeling and Decorating

- Looking for an inexpensive, one-of-a-kind headboard for your bed? Try salvaging an interesting old **door** (interior or exterior). At roughly eighty inches, when mounted horizontally to the wall behind the bed, most standard doors are the perfect length for a king-sized headboard. They also look fine with a queen-sized bed, or they can easily be trimmed a little on both ends to make them a better fit.

- And once you've repurposed an old door as a bed headboard, don't forget about the old **window frames**. They're a unique alternative to traditional picture frames, both for displaying paintings or photographs, or converting into mirrors. Particularly window frames made for multiple panes of glass make interesting mirrors or allow you to display multiple objects or images, like maybe a display of old **greeting cards,** or **postcards**, or **fabric remnants** you might otherwise throw away.

- If you have a spare picture frame, but nothing to put in it, consider filling the frame with a collection of things that reflect your interests or life. One of our favorites is a frame filled with **matchbooks** we've collected during our world travels, and a frame in my office displays my collection of strange **business cards** I've received over the years. Or maybe frame the **corks** from wines you've enjoyed, or the **bottle caps** of different beers you've tried, or colorful **buttons** you've collected.

- Add textures and designs to painting and plastering projects with some favorite repurposed items, including used **aluminum foil**, **plastic wrap**, and **pantyhose**. Simply use as a pad in applying and/or texturizing paint and plaster for a more interesting effect. Also keep old foil and plastic wrap handy when painting to wrap your paintbrushes and rollers in during a lunch break and for masking doorknobs and other fixtures you don't want painted.

- You don't need to be either an interior designer or an electrician to make one-of-a-kind lamps for decorating throughout the home. All you need is a simple "lamp kit" sold at most hardware and home improvement stores and, of course, some stuff that you might otherwise throw away. Simple canister-style lamps can be made by duct taping together **coffee cans** or other **tin cans** (with the appropriate tops/bottoms removed or left intact) to achieve the desired height and then covering with **fabric or wallpaper remnants** to accent the decor of different rooms. With a little ingenuity and the right tools, a multitude of other throwaway items can be turned into unique lamps, including old **tea and coffee pots**, **wine and other bottles**, **pieces of driftwood**, and old **vases and crockery ware** (even if cracked). And here's a really simple one to make: Glue two **clay flowerpots** together (mouth to mouth, equal in diameter), and run the lamp works through the preexisting holes in the top and bottom—you can even use a third flowerpot as a lampshade, if desired.

## Hang Your Worthless Memories on the Wall

When "Big Red"—the Raleigh ten-speed I bought in 1973 and pedaled more than fifty thousand miles over the remainder of that decade—finally and unequivocally needed to be retired, it was by every financial measure absolutely worthless.

Over the years, the once seemingly indestructible steel frame had to be spot-welded back together in half a dozen places. The wheels were so bent and out-of-true that I looked like a drunken sailor pedaling down the road. The leather saddle had become mummified, like a Ripley's Believe It or Not–worthy death mask of my butt.

Even the hardened alloy handlebars were showing the signs of tiny stress fractures, something that raced through my mind whenever I raced down a hill at thirty-plus miles an hour. What *does* a cyclist do if his handlebars choose a moment like that to break in two?

Suffice it to say that Big Red had no resale value whatsoever, even as scrap metal. And in its un-road-worthy condition, giving it away or donating it to charity would be criminal.

Yep, Big Red was worthless. But it was one of the most precious things I'd ever owned. For me, it had as many memories associated with it as it had miles behind it. There was no way I could ever part with it, let alone just throw it away.

After trying for a couple of years to avoid eye contact with my abandoned mighty steed, sadly hanging from a hook in the garage like a forgotten sack of laundry, one day I had an epiphany: *Big Red is a work of art. That frame is worthy of framing!*

I quickly constructed a crude but attractive enough "frame" out of **scrap lumber**, stapled an old **bedsheet** on one side to serve as a backdrop, and then hung the stripped-down bike frame with wire in the sort of giant shadow box. When I mounted the whole thing on the wall in my office and directed a small spotlight on it, it was—at least to my eye—one of the most beautiful works of art I'd ever seen.

But that was only the beginning of my Big Red makeover project. I mounted the front sprocket on an old oak kitchen cutting board and then installed a small battery-powered set of clockworks behind it to make the perfect wall clock for my office. I cleaned up the greasy rear sprocket (a.k.a. the "freewheel") and made it into a cool paperweight/penholder for my desk. I riveted apart the old bicycle chain and reconfigured it to spell out my name on a nameplate, now also proudly displayed on my desk.

Even the dangerously worn-out handlebars were easily and cleverly repurposed: I just set them on a shelf (with handlebar tape and brake levers left intact), and use them as bookends. The stress fractures shouldn't be a problem, unless, of course, I use them to prop up multiple copies of *War and Peace*.

I have plans to turn Big Red's wheels into a pair of garden chandeliers for the patio using twinkly lights, and I'm still ruminating over the best reuses for the pedals and what's left of that sadomasochistic leather saddle, but I'm sure something will come to me. After all, I owe it to Big Red.

No, I'm not suggesting that everyone hang a rusty old **bicycle** on their living room wall. But everyone has a Big Red of their own: something that's no longer usable but that you can't bear to part with. Maybe it's an old **sewing machine and cabinet** . . . I once saw one made into a nifty foldout liquor cabinet. Maybe it's a **canoe** with a saucer-sized hole in it . . . try cutting it in half and making a pair of matching bookshelves out of it. Or maybe it's Grandpa's broken **fishing rod**, or the **steering wheel** from your first car, or Great-Aunt Betty's **petticoat** . . . all things that can easily be displayed as interesting, highly personal works of art in your home, rather than hidden away or—worse yet—

thrown away.

When it comes to creatively repurposing items as decorations for your home, remember what Henry David Thoreau said: "It's not what you look at that matters, it's what you see."

# Chapter 3
## Kitchen and Bath

**Answer:** *My favorite thing is to use them as toilet paper. They're septic tank safe, and as expensive as toilet paper is nowadays, a very cheap alternative.*
Barry G. (Wheeling, West Virginia)

**Question**: *How do you reuse out-of-date **phone books**?* (Barry G. says it usually takes him about two months to rip through an area code.)

Even though I love Asian culture and art—particularly the minimalism and multifunctionality common in Asian design—I've never been entirely convinced about the whole *feng shui* thing.

You know, that's the ancient Chinese art of aesthetics and design intended to improve your life by receiving more positive energy and deflecting negative energy. It always seems to come down to things like which direction your house faces (not an easy fix if it's already pointed the wrong way) and the idea of having three of everything, all aligned according to a prescribed axis. I wonder if that principle of three applies to a creative re-purposer like Mike Hammond (mikehammond.com) of Walla Walla, Washington, and the giant "muffler men" he's famous for making out of junked exhaust systems salvaged from his Melody Muffler automotive shop?

Sure, feng shui is in fact an ancient and highly respected practice, but it all seems a bit too new-age-ish for a guy like me. After all, I'm the same guy who wears a beer can hat and suggests that you tinkle around the bushes in your yard to keep deer from nibbling on them. Suffice it to say, feng shui is little too foo foo for me.

But I did pick up a book about feng shui at the library the other day, primarily because it had some pretty pictures in it. I happened to flip it open to a chapter where the author, a feng shui master, was talking about how the water drains and plumbing fixtures in your house, if not properly positioned, can "drain the wealth from your life."

*Wow!* I said to myself. *Maybe there's something to this feng shui stuff after all!* You see, I've always believed that we spend more money and waste more resources in our kitchens and bathrooms—the two rooms that most commonly have plumbing fixtures and water drains—than in any other rooms in the house.

*Maybe, just maybe,* I thought, *I need to put on my beer can hat and take a closer look at how our kitchens and baths are draining our wealth.*

## Kitchen Kitsch

Here are some my favorite money-saving repurposing tips for in and around the kitchen:

- Save the **plastic mesh bags** that onions come in and stuff them inside one another to use as a handy scrubbing pad in the kitchen sink.

- A single two-liter **plastic soda bottle** can be turned into two handy kitchen gadgets: Cut off the base (about two inches from the bottom) and use it as you would a lemon/citrus juicer—the rippled plastic on the inside is perfect for wringing every drop of juice out of lemons and oranges. Then trim the top portion to the desired size and use as a kitchen funnel.

- Pages torn out of an old **phone book** or **yellow pages** come in handy as kitchen wipes and for separating baked goods and other items in the freezer.

- Have you ever tried to tear open a plastic **cereal bag** with your bare hands? Most are incredibly tough these days, so I usually end up cutting them open. And that's exactly why cereal bags should be washed, saved, and reused: They're the toughest bags around for storing leftovers in or for other general household use.

- Get double duty out of a **watermelon rind** by hollowing it out to make an all-natural serving "basket" for a fruit salad before you later turn it into pickled watermelon rind (see Chapter

4) or send it off to the compost pile. Similarly, scoop the meat out of acorn **squash** halves and use the **shells** as serving bowls for a tasty squash soup.

- I've never understood why people buy special containers to store leftovers and other food in (Tupperware sales alone were $2.3 billion in 2010 . . . no wonder they're having so many parties!). If you look in most people's trash or recycling bin on any given week, I'll bet dollars to donuts you'll find all types of containers that recently and very successfully stored food. Hang on to a varied supply of nicely made **glass and plastic jars and bottles** to store food and other items in, and you'll be hanging on to a good deal more of your own money when you do.

- Keep a couple of empty **CD cases** on hand in the kitchen to hold recipe cards while you're cooking to keep them splatter free. It's also a convenient way to organize and store groups of related recipe cards.

- **Lemon rinds** and other **citrus rinds** just smell way too good to throw away. Boil them in water on the stove top or microwave them for a minute for an all-natural air freshener in the kitchen. And put a couple in the humidifier to make the whole house smell lemony fresh. Lemon and other citrus rinds can also be used to make copper pots and pans shine—just use them as a scrub pad with a little baking soda.

- Store potatoes, onions, and garlic in old pairs of **pantyhose** and hang them in the pantry to promote good air circulation that will make your veggies last longer. Pantyhose can also be used in the kitchen to strain foods through instead of cheesecloth. Yes, of course you'll want to thoroughly launder them first.

- And don't even get me started about **aluminum foil**—the Aluminum Association says we buy 1.3 billion pounds of it every year! Think of how many leftover meatballs that represents. Of course aluminum foil can be cleaned, flattened out—I use my rolling pin on the kitchen counter—and used again. (Caution: Foil that has come in contact with raw meat should not be reused for other food purposes.) Or wad it up in a ball for cleaning the gunk off the BBQ grill and stuck-on food from pots, pans, and oven racks. Used foil is also handy for lining roasting pans and cookie sheets.

- Unwanted **clay flowerpots** provide a clever way to bake and serve fresh bread, particularly smaller pots used for individual-sized servings. Just grease the inside of a pot (cleaned thoroughly, of course) and let a ball of bread dough—frozen or freshly made—rise in it, then bake according to your favorite recipe.

- Fill empty **plastic soda bottles** nearly full with water and keep them in your freezer. A full freezer is more energy efficient and will stay colder for longer if you lose power. Plus you can use the frozen bottles as "dripless ice cubes" when you pack your ice chest for a family outing.

- Shake crushed **eggshells** and a little soapy water to scour hard-to-clean items like thermoses and vases. Crushed eggshells can also be used as a nontoxic abrasive on pots and pans. And keep a couple of crushed eggshells in your kitchen sink strainer at all times; they trap solids and gradually break up and help to naturally clean your pipes on their way down the drain.

- Sterilize "blown out" **eggshells** (see Chapter 5) in boiling water or by steaming them, and then carefully fill them with Jell-O or chocolate to make unique egg-shaped treats (sealing off one of the pinholes with plastic tape). Peel away the eggshell mold before serving, or serve as is and let your guests discover the surprise inside.

- Cover **coffee cans** and **oatmeal containers** with leftover **wallpaper** or **fabric remnants** to make matching canisters for storing flour, sugar, salt, and so forth, on the kitchen counter.

- Cloth dish rags made from **fabric remnants** and old **clothing**, **towels**, or even **bedsheets** can easily save the average family more than $100 per year compared to using paper towels (per my calculations). But if you do use **paper**

**towels**, reuse them by "speed drying" them with a couple of centrifugal whirls in a salad spinner; the same method can be used to dry **plastic bags**, **plastic wrap**, and **aluminum foil** for reuse.

- Growing up, in my family our "everyday" glasses were always a collection of old jelly jars. In fact, I didn't even know that you could buy so-called juice glasses until I left home, as I recall. Maybe most folks are too sophisticated to drink out of jelly jars or Mason jars these days, but "bottle cutting kits" available online and elsewhere (starting at about $25) let you make a wide variety of really cool glasses and vases out of **glass bottles and jars**. That's less than you'd probably pay for a set of glasses, and making them is easy and fun. They make great gifts, too.

## Shocking Eco Facts

*Drip, drip, drip.* That's not just the sound of money going down the drain. Water—particularly freshwater—is quickly becoming one of Earth's scarcest resources because we're using and wasting so much of it. According to the World Water Council (worldwatercouncil.org), an international nonprofit organization dedicated to addressing concerns about world water issues on a global basis, 1.1 billion people live without clean drinking water, and nearly 4,000 children die every day from waterborne disease. Daily per capita residential use of water in the United States and Japan is nearly twice as much as in Europe, and more than twenty times that of people living in sub-Saharan Africa. At current usage rates, experts predict that between one-half and two-thirds of the world's population will face severe freshwater shortages within the next twenty-five years. In the United States, we each use about eighty to one hundred gallons of water per day for personal purposes, with most of it being flushed down the toilet (baths/showers are the second-highest use). If you don't think a drop here or there adds up, check out this "drip calculator" to see how much that leaky faucet or toilet is really wasting: ga.water.usgs.gov/edu/sc4.html.

## Bath, Beauty, and Beyond

Commonly thrown away items can help you save money in the bathroom, as well as make you more beautiful and even cure some common ailments. Check out these powder room tips.

**Simple Toilet Tank Trick:** Now that you know how much water—and money—you're literally flushing down the drain, that **plastic soda bottle** you were getting ready to throw away can help you save both. Just put a plastic bottle or two filled with water into your toilet tank, and you'll displace enough water to save half a gallon to a gallon with every flush. Most toilets flush just fine with a little less water. Based on my calculations of average FPP's ("Flushes Per Person"), a family of four will save about sixteen gallons of water a day with this little trick, which should save about $90 a year on their water bill.

**Potpourri for the Potty:** I love my wife, but she knows that nothing sets me off like store-bought potpourri for the bathroom and other places around the house. (I have the world's largest supply of that stuff in the back-yard . . . it's in my compost pile!) All types of **citrus rinds**, **apple peels**, **pomegranate skins**, **rose petals**, and **other fruit and flower trimmings** can simply be dried on a rack to make homemade potpourri. Sprinkle a little "liquid potpourri" (available at craft stores) on it for more flavor if desired, or dose it with the dregs of perfume or cologne when you finish up a bottle.

**Is That Peach Fuzz on Your Face?:** Peaches are high in vitamin A and potassium, which help to revitalize skin and keep it hydrated. Put a little sugar on the pulpy side of **peach skins** and use as a gentle face scrub.

**Pomegranate Skin to Relieve Diarrhea:** Boil a little **pomegranate skin** in water with a cinnamon stick and drink it down while it's still warm. Repeat up to three times per day or until diarrhea subsides.

**Call Me Mr. Potato Head:** To naturally darken your hair, boil **potato peels** in water for about a half hour, then strain and let cool. Rinse your hair with this water after shampooing and it will gradually darken gray hair, without the use of harsh chemicals. (Rinse, repeat, and add gravy, as needed.)

**Spoil Your Skin with a Spoiled Yogurt and Cucumber Peel: Yogurt** that is past its prime is one of only a few spoiled dairy products that is difficult to reuse creatively in cooking (see Chapter 4), but the good news is it makes a soothing face mask. In a blender, mix one cup spoiled yogurt with any **cucumber peels** you have to spare, and a dollop of honey if you really want to get salon-fancy. Apply liberally to your face and leave it on for thirty minutes before washing it off. Of course leftover **egg whites** also make an excellent skin-tightening face mask.

**Soap Grime Fighter:** The same chemicals used in **fabric dryer sheets** to make clothes softer also make them good wipes to use in removing soap scum from bathtubs, showers, and tiles. Even once you've used them in the dryer, they still have plenty of grime-fighting power left.

**Are Your Dogs Killing You?:** Rub **papaya skins and pulp** on the bottoms of your feet to help soften skin and soothe cracked heels. Papaya is rich in vitamin A and papain, which breaks down inactive proteins and removes dead skin cells. (Plus it feels pretty cool.

**Even Thinner Than an Eggshell:** The superthin **membrane *inside* the eggshell** has long been used as a home remedy for a wide range of ailments, including healing cuts, treating ingrown toenails, and even clearing up pimples. Simply apply the membrane to the skin as you would a very thin bandage.

**Treat Skin Irritations:** Dissolve an **eggshell** in a small jar of apple cider vinegar (takes about two days) and apply the mixture to treat minor skin irritations and itchy skin. (It would probably taste pretty good on a salad, too.)

**Rub-a-Dub-Dub, There's a Cheapskate in My Tub!:** Save those little **slivers of soap** and put them in the feet of a pair of worn-out **pantyhose** to get every last bit of suds out of them. I call it my "Cheapskate-Soap-on-a-Rope" and I wear it around my neck when I shower, which my wife thinks is pretty sexy. I also keep one tied to the outdoor water faucet for a quick cleanup after working in the yard.

**Save the Slivers:** If a Cheapskate-Soap-on-a-Rope isn't your style, leftover **slivers of soap** can also be transformed back into fresh bars. Put the slivers in a cooking pot, add just enough water to cover them, and then let them sit for a day, stirring from time to time. Heat the mixture slowly on the stove, stirring until the mixture is smooth and lump free. Stir in one tablespoon of vegetable oil for every cup of the mixture, and then pour the mixture into lightly oiled molds, small dishes, or even small **cardboard boxes** (matchboxes work well) lined with repurposed **wax paper.** Allow to cool and dry. Ratchet up the repurposing even more by stirring into the mixture any **leftover oatmeal**, grated **citrus**

**rinds**, and/or pulverizing **pistachio shells** or other **nutshells** you might have on hand. You can also add food coloring if you're color conscious about your re-purposed soap.

**Or Make a Dirty Snowball:** For a quicker fix, you can also melt **soap slivers** in a lightly oiled dish in the microwave, zapping them for thirty seconds at a time until they start to melt together. Remove from oven, stir them up a bit, and as soon as the mixture is cool enough to handle, mold them by hand into what can only be described as "dirty snowballs." Once they fully cool, they get the job done, though.

**And Last But Not Least:** My great-grandmother would make a "bread and milk poultice" by pouring warm milk on **stale bread** wrapped in a bandage or towel, then applying it to an afflicted area to bring boils and abscesses to a head. She claimed it really worked. If you try it and it does, afterward you have my permission to finally "Throw That Sh*t Away!"

## More Nifty-Thrifty Repurposing Tips for Kitchen and Bath

- Cover old **phone books** in **fabric remnants** to make attractive little boosters to help kids sit up at the dinner table.

- Glue **foam packing peanuts** on magnets and use with push pins to tack the grocery list and other notes to the door of the fridge. Let the kids make a set of their own—complete with glue-on "bug eyes" and **twisty-seal** legs—as their own personal message boards.

- Here's a bathroom-to-kitchen crossover repurposing tip from one of my Miser Advisers: When she remodeled her bathroom, she installed the old **medicine cabinet** in her kitchen as a perfect place to store spices and canned goods. She liked it so much that she's now added a couple more medicine cabinets to her kitchen pantry, all found at yard sales and thrift stores.

- Keep freshly baked cookies soft for longer by storing them with a slice of **stale bread** in an airtight container. This storage method will also keep brown sugar from hardening in the pantry. Stale = Fresh. Who knew?

- **Old CDs and DVDs** make conversation-starting drink coasters; glue felt on the flip side to trap moisture and avoid scratching the surface underneath.

- The elastic band cut from a pair of old men's **underwear** (that's underwear that is old, not necessarily underwear previously worn by an old man) works well for keeping plastic trash bags from disappearing into wastebaskets in the kitchen and bath. Use an old **bicycle inner tube** for this same purpose on larger trash cans, just in case you don't wear underwear with a seventy-five-inch waist.

- Speaking of trash bags, true cheapskates are appalled at the very thought of buying a bag for the express purpose of throwing it away. Reuse **plastic shopping bags**, **paper bags**, and **big bags like pet food comes in** as trash bags rather than buying regular garbage bags at the store—that's rubbish.

- Repurpose **gift wrapping paper** by smoothing it out and laminating it or covering it with clear contact paper to use as everyday placemats or kitchen/bath shelf liners. **Wallpaper remnants** also make terrific shelf lining.

- Keep an old **disposable razor** (sterilized in boiling water, of course) on hand in the kitchen to remove fine hairs from chicken and other poultry that needs a shave.

- And finally, another repurposing double-header: I love the smell of frying bacon when I'm working in the kitchen, so much so that I made a bacon-scented kitchen candle by simply pouring leftover **bacon grease** (also see Chapter 4) into an empty **tin can** and inserting a cloth wick. It burns great and fills the whole room with the smell of frying bacon. *That's* my kind of aroma therapy.

### Bottoms Up!

It's only fitting that the Chinese—the very same culture that invented the ancient art of feng shui—have applied some of those same design principles in increasingly creative ways in the new millennium.

With feng shui's emphasis on water and preventing

wealth and positive energy from literally being flushed down the drain, I suppose it was only a matter of time before "toilet restaurants" emerged to delight enthusiastic Sino diners.

At toilet restaurants that are springing up throughout China and now beginning to spread across Asia (it's a growing *movement*, that's for sure), restaurant patrons are seated on repurposed porcelain **commodes** and eat off tables fashioned from old **bathroom sinks, tubs,** and even **urinals.** Of course none of the plumbing fixtures are functional, both to prevent positive energy and wealth from being drained from the dining establishment, as well as discourage customers from leaving an unwelcome tip at the table in the event of unsatisfactory service.

Okay, so maybe everyone's not ready to take the plunge and decorate their dining room in modern Kohler or early American Standard toilet furnishings, but unwanted **toilet** bowls do make whimsical planters for the garden (you can plant flowers and/or veggies in both the bowl and the tank), as do **kitchen and bathroom sinks**. And since dogs love drinking out of them anyhow, consider converting an old toilet or sink into a pet watering bowl or birdbath.

Over seven million unwanted toilets end up in U.S. landfills every year. Check with your local municipal recycler to see if it can recycle them instead (they're commonly crushed up and used in concrete or as fill—see Chapter 7). Also, many older toilets—even ones like those avocado green models from the 1970s—have a fairly high resale value through architectural salvage stores specializing in vintage building materials.

# Chapter 4
## Food

**Answer:** *I save them up in a bag in the freezer until I have enough to use to bake a cake or coffee cake with them. They're also really good in pancakes or muffins. They add such a great texture and flavor.*
Martha D. (Stockton, California)

**Question:** *What can you do with* **bread crumbs** *salvaged from your toaster or the catch tray in your toaster oven?* (As Martha D. says, "Why do you think they call it 'crumb cake'?")

Be forewarned that if I ever visit your home, I'm not likely to sneak a peek in your medicine cabinet, as many houseguests are suspected of doing. But when you're not looking, I might very well do some pantry peeping. You can tell a lot about a family by looking in their refrigerator, freezer, and food cupboards.

My fixation with people's food caches began in my childhood, when I noticed that my grandma Yeager kept some pretty strange things in her kitchen, particularly in her freezer.

In fairness, much of it was normal enough foodstuff, although some of it was rather old. For example, in her freezer she kept a slice of wedding **cake** from her great-aunt's wedding. Nellie was married during Grover Cleveland's second term. During the sixty-plus years the slice of cake had remained more or less cryogenically preserved (first in the family's "icebox," and later in Grandma's electric "deep freeze"), the frosting had mysteriously yellowed in such a way that a perfect profile image of our twenty-fourth president could be seen if the slice was held in just the right light. Oh, if only eBay had existed back then.

But there were other, even more bizarre, *non*-foodstuffs in Grandma Yeager's deep freeze.

She kept her spare **batteries** in there because it made them last longer. And her supply of wax **candles** because it made them burn longer. Packets of **seeds** spent the winter in the freezer to help them germinate more successfully come springtime, and she always kept her **nylon stockings** in the freezer, insisting that it made them less likely to run (and they felt "Oh Godfrey . . . so refreshing!" when she slipped them on).

Once, I even found one of Grandpa's **wooden duck decoys** in the freezer. It was showing the telltale pinholes of a woodworm infestation, and apparently all members of the Greatest Generation were born with the knowledge that deep freezing is a surefire way to rid your duck decoys of woodworms.

And Grandma put her damp laundry in a plastic bag as soon as it came out of the wash and then stuck it in the freezer. It kept the clothes from getting moldy and made them easier to iron, or so she claimed.

Her biggest deep frozen secret of all, though, was a **plastic bread wrapper** containing her "mad money," usually hidden safely within her bag of frozen laundry. I remember once when I was a kid, Grams went to pay me for mowing her lawn. She peeled a stiff $5 bill off her frozen girdle in the icebox and handed it over to me. And you wonder why I still have issues?

My grandmother's strange freezer habits aside, what you'll find when you look in most people's refrigerators, freezers, and food pantries is a lot of food going to waste. Clearly we need to be smarter about food storage and preservation, as well as portion control. But there are also ways you can repurpose—as in still consume—foodstuffs that you might otherwise throw away.

### Shocking Eco Facts

According to the Environmental Protection Agency (EPA.gov), food leftovers are the single largest component by weight of everything we throw away in the United States. That includes food scraps from households as well as commercial establishments like restaurants and other industrial sources. Wasted food accounts for over 12 percent of the solid waste by the typical American household, which adds up to 31 million tons annually. That's roughly equivalent to the weight of seventy-four Golden Gate Bridges, so says a related article in *USA Today*. Wow, talk about a mouthful! To make matters worse, decomposing food and other organic matter in landfills produces methane, a greenhouse gas twenty-one times more damaging to the environment than carbon dioxide. Plus, we spend almost $1 billion every year just to dispose of our leftovers. Mom knew best: Always clean your plate.

## Meat and Dairy Products

No, I'm not suggesting that you eat rotten meat (although in Chapter 7 you'll find an alternative or two to simply throwing it away). But there is some perfectly edible animal protein that most people throw away as a matter of course, which could instead be saved and consumed.

**Animal Fat:** To get right to the fat of the matter, congealed **animal fat** left over after cooking all types of meats—beef, pork, lamb, even poultry—is considered a delicacy in many parts of the world and has a number of cooking uses in any kitchen. **Pork fat** is typically rendered into lard, but any congealed animal fat that has been properly stored can be used in a similar fashion as an alternative to vegetable-based oils when frying or baking foods.

Because animal fat is admittedly less healthy than most vegetable-based oils—though it's also generally much more flavorful—I prefer to use it sparingly as an oil substitute in cooking, incorporating it into dishes where its flavor really stands out. For example, **bacon fat** adds wonderful flavor to steamed greens or when poured hot over fresh spinach to make a wilted spinach salad, further dressed with sweetened vinegar. Eggs fried in leftover bacon fat are heavenly. And if you're a fellow fan of Yorkshire pudding, you know that **beef fat** or even **lamb fat** ignites a flavor fest in what otherwise would be a pretty bland dish.

**Bones and Shells:** It's interesting that we no longer do much when it comes to repurposing **bones**. Prior to the twentieth century, bones were one of the most commonly recycled items, according to Susan Strasser's fascinating book *Waste and Want: A Social History of Trash*. They were used for everything from making buttons, glue, and paper to multiple applications in food processing and even photography.

In the modern kitchen, **bones** of all varieties—mammal, fish, and fowl—can still be used to make flavorful stock. The best stock is usually made by first baking the bones (400-degree oven for about thirty minutes, depending on the size/type of bones) to enhance the flavor and help break down the flesh, fat, marrow, and cartilage. Ideally, larger bones should be cut into smaller pieces to help release the marrow and other flavors. Once roasted, the bones are then simmered in a stockpot (again, cooking times vary) until the flavor is fully extracted. Smaller bones rendered in this way are then usually okay to put in the compost pile.

On a related note, **shrimp shells** (including the heads and tails) make an excellent and quick stock as well, or they can be fried or baked as is done in Japan and eaten as a crispy snack. Don't turn up your nose: A 2007 study published in the journal *Clinical and Experimental Pharmacology and Physiology* showed that a chemical called chitosan found in shrimp shells might be beneficial in fighting both obesity and high cholesterol.

**Offal:** And finally, there's no greater waste of perfectly tasty animal protein than the contents of that little paper sack most people pluck from the cavity of the turkeys and other poultry they buy, only to deposit it directly in the trash can. I speak, of course, of the infamous *baggie o' giblets* containing the neck, liver, heart, gizzard, and other anything-but-awful **offal** of the bird.

According to the U.S. Department of Agriculture, more than forty-five million turkeys are cooked and eaten in the United States at Thanksgiving alone. By my calculations, that means that we're spending more than $30 million on giblets at Thanksgiving, most of which are thrown away. Nutritionally, that represents more than forty billion calories, or enough to feed roughly fifty-five thousand people for an entire year (provided, of course, you could find fifty-five thousand people longing for an all-giblet diet).

In addition to using them to make stock (above), adding them to your favorite stuffing recipe, or making traditional giblet gravy, I like to use the contents of the baggie o' giblets to make a simple pâté. First simmer all the parts in water until fully cooked, and then remove the meat from the neck and any hard portions from the offal. Combine the meat with a little chopped onion, sherry, and butter in a food processor, and blend until smooth, adding more butter as needed. Serve as canapé on crackers or small rounds of toast, and you'll never pitch a baggie o' giblets again.

When it comes to salvaging dairy products that are past their prime, there are a few options to consider, particularly if you're a somewhat adventuresome eater.

**Sour Milk:** Many experienced bakers insist that using milk that has begun to spoil or "sour" is preferable when cooking recipes for breads, biscuits, and other baked goods that call for buttermilk or "soured milk" (which is milk that has intentionally been soured by adding lemon juice or vinegar). Spoiled milk can also be used to make "paneer," a traditional farmer's cheese from India that is a key ingredient in Indian cuisine. Here's a recipe for paneer made with spoiled milk: youtube.com/watch?v=776I-YD6jDo.

**Spoiled Yogurt:** Some foodies claim they use spoiled yogurt in baking, to replace soured milk when called for in a recipe, as discussed above. But why risk wasting some perfectly good spoiled yogurt when you can instead use it as a skin-rejuvenating face mask (see Chapter 3)?

**Moldy Cheese:** The Holy Trinity of eternal questions: *The meaning of life? What happens after you die? Is moldy cheese safe to eat?* According to this article written by Katherine Zeratsky, a nutritionist with the Mayo Clinic, mayoclinic.com/health/food-and-nutrition/AN01024, it all depends on the type of cheese. In general, softer cheeses like cream cheese, cottage cheese, and brie should not be eaten once they show signs of mold. However, many harder cheeses, including cheddar, Swiss, and gorgonzola are safe to eat if you adequately trim away the moldy portions. See the article for a listing of cheeses that are safe/not safe to eat when moldy, as well as additional instructions.

**Spoiled Butter:** The good news is, butter (particularly salted butter) is relatively slow to spoil, even if it's left unrefrigerated for a little while. Once butter has turned rancid, the smell and even a small taste will immediately let you know. While some adventuresome repurposer chefs claim that you can restore rancid butter by soaking in a solution of baking soda, I say *"Butter* to be safe, rather than sorry" and don't risk it. This may be a case where you really should *throw that away*, although FYI when butter spoils, it produces butyric acid, which reeks to high heaven and is sometimes used by protesters and others to make homemade stink bombs.

**Rotten Eggs:** A truly "bad egg" will announce itself as soon as you crack it open, both with its trademarked "rotten egg smell" and runny consistency. Although eggs are very often safe to consume well beyond the "sell by" date printed on the carton (according to the USDA, if properly stored, eggs often remain fresh three to five weeks beyond the sell by date), once they've spoiled they're both unsafe and unsavory to consume. But don't get down in the yolks about it, because rotten eggs can always be repurposed in the garden (see Chapter 7).

**Spoiled Sour Cream:** *How can sour cream go sour?* Sounds like a George Carlin routine, doesn't it? But indeed sour cream can spoil and grow moldy. And when it does, even the most creative repurposers say it's finally time to *Throw That Away!*

## Bread and Grains

I've often thought of writing an entire book devoted to ways to repurpose **stale bread**. If I ever do, I'll dedicate it to my great-grandmother. She was born to a peasant family in Czechoslovakia and grew up eating crusty European-style bread that had further turned to stone and was handed out for free to needy families after it was too old and stale to sell. As a result, my great-grandmother actually developed a fondness for stale bread. Plus she had more tricks for reusing stale bread than there are slices in a loaf.

Even once she moved to America and could afford fresh bread, Great-Grandma found it wholly unsatisfying. That's when she took to buying fresh bread and laying out the slices all over her kitchen to make her own stale bread. Sure, her house always smelled like a brewery, but now I have to admit that stale bread really should be treasured, not trashed.

You can revive stale bread and make it soft again by wrapping it in a moist paper towel and microwaving it for thirty seconds or so. But that would just break my great-grandmother's heart. Instead, consider using it to make the following.

**Bread Crumbs:** Give stale bread a whirl in the blender or food processor along with some Italian seasonings for the freshest-stale bread crumbs ever. Store in an airtight container in the fridge.

**Bread Puddings:** Everybody's great-grandmother had her favorite bread pudding recipe. In the fall, I like to add some pumpkin and dried cranberries to mine.

**Bread Salads:** A classic Mediterranean dish. Toss an ample amount of stale bread cubes in with tomatoes, olives, lettuces, and other fresh vegetables, dress with olive oil and wine vinegar, and you can make an entire dinner out of this simple salad.

**Bread Soups:** So-called bread soups are a hardy dinnertime staple in countries around the globe, and for good reason—they're delicious and cheap. My favorite is this tomato-bread soup: epicurious.com/recipes/food/views/Tomato-and-Bread-Soup-15614.

**Breakfast Cereal?!:** That's right. Great-Grandma loved stale bread with brown sugar and milk on it in lieu of store-bought breakfast cereal. I told you she was a true stale bread aficionado.

**French Toast:** A more conventional use of stale bread for breakfast. In fact, French toast was originally invented as a way to use up stale bread. Try using stale bread instead of fresh for your favorite French toast recipe and you'll be amazed by how much tastier it is.

**Garlic Bread:** Rub stale bread with garlic and olive oil, then bake for the best garlic bread ever. Or try stale bread bruschetta topped with chopped tomatoes, onion, and olives on the grill.

**Grilled Cheese Sandwiches:** Start with stale bread rather than fresh and your grilled cheese sandwiches and panini will be even crispier.

**Croutons:** Sauté cubes of stale bread in olive oil and/ or butter with a little Parmesan cheese, and you'll never eat croutons from a box again.

**Meatloaf Mop:** Put a layer of stale bread in the bottom of the dish to soak up excess fat when baking a meatloaf or roasting other greasy meats.

**Stuffing:** Cubed or crumbed stale bread works just as well in your favorite stuffing recipe as fresh.

**Thicken Sauces:** Sauces, soups, and stews can be thickened simply by stirring in stale bread crumbs.

**Salud!:** My great-grandma was a proud teetotaler, although she didn't consider Russian "kvass"—a light beer-like drink made with stale bread—to be alcoholic, since it typically has an alcohol content of only around 1 percent. She'd make it by putting a slice of stale bread in a cup of water, let it sit for a day, strain out the bread, then add two tablespoons of sugar and two tablespoons of yeast starter along with a few raisins. When the raisins float, it's ready to drink. (Just for the record, *kvass* means "acid" in Polish, so proceed at your own risk.)

Bread isn't the only grain product that can be resurrected and consumed in some form or fashion if it's a little past its prime or you have some leftover.

How many times have you emptied day-old **rice** from the Chinese carryout into the trash and marveled at how it had morphed into a hard brick the same shape as the box it came in? Rest assured that I'm experimenting in the Ultimate Cheapskate Lab with possible home construction applications for repurposing that starchy stuff, but in the meantime freeze leftover cooked rice to use the next time you make soup, rice pudding, or any other recipe that calls for cooked rice. As an ingredient in dishes like those, it works just as well as freshly made rice. It can also be used to make stir-fried rice, or eaten hot or cold as a breakfast cereal with sugar, cinnamon, and milk—it's really quite delicious.

Speaking of breakfast cereal, stale or soggy **cereal**, **crackers**, and **chips** can be refreshed by spreading them out on a cookie sheet and baking them in a 425-degree oven for a few minutes, or by putting them in a damp paper bag (loosely closed) and blasting them in the microwave for ten seconds at a time, until rejuvenated. Stale cereals like Cheerios and Chex can also be lightly fried in butter or margarine and salt and served as a snack. All these stale items can be made into crumbs in the food processor or blender and used in place of bread crumbs in most recipes.

And finally, what if you have some **oatmeal** in the cupboard that you think might be past its prime? Don't be too hasty: While it's possible for oatmeal to go bad, a few years ago scientists at Brigham Young University tested rolled oats that had been stored for twenty-eight years in a sealed container and found them to not only be edible, but still pretty tasty.

## Shut Up and Eat Your Compost

More than once my pooooor wife has sent me out to the compost pile with the **coffee can** we keep in the kitchen to collect fruit and veggie scraps, only to have me return with the can still full, convinced that there's still plenty of good eating to be had in that can. Sure, a whole lot of those peels and other trimmings can be simmered in water to make a tasty vegetable stock, but here are some other ways to *eat your compost*:

- Candied citrus rinds were one of the first things I learned how to cook when I was a kid, and I still love to make a batch to nibble on after dinner. Just boil strips of rind from **lemons**, **oranges**, **grapefruits**, and **limes** in a mixture of equal parts water and sugar until the liquid is absorbed (a couple of hours).

Coat the cooled strips in granulated or powdered sugar and let dry on a rack.

- All kinds o' rinds can also be pickled and eaten as a delicious condiment. Most recipes for pickled **watermelon**, **lemon**, **orange**, and even **pumpkin rind** (see sidebar) involve a simple mixture of vinegar, sugar, and spices. Once prepared, most can just be stored in the fridge rather than canned.

- Marmalades are simple to make, even for those new to jam cookery. They can incorporate the skins from a wide variety of fruits—not just **oranges**, but **lemons**, **grapefruit**, **limes**, **tangerines**, and even **kumquats**. The website pickyourown.org offers good recipes and advice for making marmalades, as well as a nationwide directory for farms where you can save even more by picking your own produce.

- Garrison Keillor once said, "Sex is good, but not as good as fresh sweet corn." I agree, even when it comes to sweet **corn husks and cobs**. I like to wrap fish and other seafood in dampened sweet corn husks, and then grill and serve them that way. And corncobs—from sweet corn or even regular field corn—can be used to make old-fashioned corncob jelly and corncob wine. Definitely better than sex, depending on . . .

- Dried tangerine rind is a tasty—and expensive—ingredient used in Asian cooking. But you can make your own by simply using a vegetable peeler to remove the orange part of the **tangerine**, **clementine**, or **tangelo rind** (avoid the white zest) and dry the peels on a rack or in a food dehydrator. Once dried, store in an airtight container in the fridge.

- All kinds of fruit skins—particularly **citrus rinds**—can be added to vodka to create a flavorful infusion. Just add the peels and let it sit for a week or two. And adding citrus peels to olive oil will not only flavor it, but it helps to reinvigorate oil that's getting old. Flavored vodkas and olive oils (attractively packaged in **glass bottles** you couldn't bear to throw away) also make terrific homemade gifts . . . no need to feel guilty about regifting your compost to someone you love.

- My mom makes delicious jelly from **apple peels**, and when I was a kid she'd sometimes dust apple skins with sugar and cinnamon and bake them in the oven as a crispy snack. That woman could teach Martha Stewart a thing or two.

- And last but not least, my favorite, *Compost Pile Chicken*. Trimmings, peels, and rinds of almost any variety—**onions**, **celery**, **carrots**, **citrus**, **apples**, **garlic**, and so on—can be stuffed inside the cavity of a whole chicken (preferably a dead one) and sprinkled around it in the roasting pan to add wonderful flavor and aroma. Once baked, the trimmings are

then ready for a proper burial in the compost
pile, where they'll break down even faster
since they've been roasted.

## More Nifty-Thrifty Repurposing Tips for Leftover Food

- *Let them eat **leftover cake**!* Even as a kid I
  didn't really like cake . . . unless it sat around
  too long and started to get stale. Then my
  mom would pour cold milk over it and serve
  it to me in a bowl, which left me lapping it up
  like a pig through hot strawberries. Don't turn
  up your nose—try it. You'll also find that slivers of almost any variety of stale cake will only
  enhance your favorite tiramisu recipe when
  substituted for the oh-so-overdone ladyfingers.

- Have a little **leftover wine** from your dinner party? That's never actually happened at
  our house, but I suppose it is a metaphysical
  possibility. Keep an ice cube tray in the freezer
  earmarked for cryogenically storing cubes of
  leftover red, white, or even sparkling wines. It
  won't really be fit for drinking, but it's a great
  way to keep leftover wine on hand for adding to soup stocks, sauces, salad dressing, and
  the like.

- Throw some **peanut shells** on the barbie. Peanut shells—and other **nutshells**—burn slow
  'n' smoky, so add a handful to the charcoal
  next time you're grilling. Soak them in water
  ahead of time if you think of it, and let them

dry a bit before you put them in the coals—
that way they'll burn even longer.

- Another egg-cellent use for **eggshells**: Add the
shell of a previously-cooked egg (hard-boiled
or soft-boiled) to the coffee in the filter before
you brew it. It will make your coffee less bit-
ter, and the spent **coffee grounds**, eggshells,
and **paper filter** are then all conveniently
ready for the compost pile.

- And whatever you do, don't throw away that
nearly empty bottle or jar of condiments before you swirl some apple cider vinegar around
in it first and then add the contents to your
trusty drippins jar in the fridge. Smidgeons of
**jams**, **jellies**, **honey**, **peanut butter**, **ketchup**,
**mustard**, **relish**, **salad dressings**, and all other
manner of **sauces and condiments** can be
dislodged from their containers in this fashion
and added to what becomes a flavorful—al-
beit always evolving—mix that can be used as
a salad dressing, marinade, or dipping sauce.
Truly good to the last drop.

### How to Eat Your Jack-o'-Lantern

"Jeff, can't we at least wait until the holiday is over before you eat the decorations?" That's my pooooor wife's
favorite line every Halloween. In addition to trying to
pop the colorful **Indian corn** she hangs on the front
door (FYI, not so successful), I have a long-standing
tradition of eating our **jack-o'-lantern**. And I mean

every last bite of it.

All pumpkins are edible—even the big ones sold for making jack-o'-lanterns—although admittedly some varieties are tastier than others. Best of all, they're inexpensive (particularly the day *after* Halloween) and they're packed with beta-carotene, a powerful antioxidant, and other vitamins and minerals. Americans buy more than one billion pounds of pumpkins at Halloween, but the vast majority of those end up in the trash. Not at the House of Cheap.

Of course lots of people save the **seeds** from their jack-o'-lantern to make a healthy snack food. Just wash the seeds, let them dry a little, then add salt and roast them on a lightly oiled cookie sheet in a 250-degree oven for an hour or so (turning as needed). I like to get creative and flavor my seeds with a lot more than just plain salt. Try making batches of designer seeds using seasoning like the following: Cajun spices; ginger powder; pumpkin pie spice; garlic salt; curry powder; chili powder; cinnamon; or vinegar and salt.

The thick, bright orange **pulp** lining the inside of the pumpkin is the real meat of the matter when it comes to making pies, cakes, bread, soups, and other pumpkin delicacies. Use a large spoon to scoop the pulp from inside, working it down to the whitish-colored layer directly beneath the skin and leaving the outer shell to carve as a jack-o'-lantern. Once you've extracted the pulp, steam it over a pot of boiling water until it's tender (about thirty minutes). Run it through a food processor or mash it by hand (add a dash of lemon juice to prevent freezer burn), and freeze in plastic bags or containers to use later in your favorite recipes for pies and other pumpkin dishes. You can also eat the cooked pulp just like squash, with salt, pepper, and butter.

I like to use freshly steamed pumpkin pulp in this Pumpkin Cider Bisque recipe I invented: Make a cream soup by melting 4 tablespoons butter and mixing in 4 tablespoons flour, and then slowly stir in 2 cups whole milk. Stir constantly over medium heat until thickened. Add 1 cup cooked pumpkin puree (see above), and heat through. Slowly add 2 cups cider. Correct the seasoning with salt and pepper. Serve hot, with a dollop of sour cream, or cold with apple slices to garnish. Delicious, healthy, and typically costs under fifty cents per serving!

If your jack-o'-lantern doesn't get smashed by neighborhood hellions and doesn't show signs of rot or excessive candle scorching, the day after Halloween is the time to pickle the **rind**.

Remove the orange outer skin with a vegetable peeler. Cut the white-colored rind into two-inch squares. Cover cubes with apple cider vinegar and let soak overnight. Remove the pumpkin from vinegar and repurpose it some other way. Let cubes dry on a rack. Make a mixture of fresh vinegar, sugar, ginger, and cinnamon, and bring to a boil on the stove. (For each pound of pumpkin, use 3/4 pound sugar, 2 cups vinegar, and a piece of fresh ginger. Add a stick of cinnamon for the whole batch of several pounds.) Add pumpkin and simmer until pieces are translucent and golden yellow, about 3 hours on low heat. Never stir with a spoon; just shake the pot occasionally so the pumpkin doesn't fall apart. Can and seal, or store in the refrigerator for up to a few weeks.

# Chapter 5
## Family Fun: Crafts, Recreation, Holidays, and More

**Answer:** *The kids and I string them together with a needle and fishing line and hang them on the Christmas tree. Sometimes we even paint and decorate them. It's fun, and—unlike popcorn and cranberries—they last for years.* Dorothy D. (Pittsburgh, Pennsylvania)

**Question:** *What can you do with those colorful **foam "peanuts"** that are used in packing boxes?*

*What's the most fun you can remember having as a kid?* Close your eyes and think about it for a minute.

If you're anywhere near my age (I'm in my mid-fifties), I'll bet that very few of the fond memories that come floating up to the top of your mind have to do with expensive toys, or lavish vacations, or holidays where you received so many gifts you needed your own Dewey Decimal system to catalog them all.

That's not to say that perhaps your childhood didn't include all those things. Certainly I enjoyed my fair share of time being coddled, celebrated, and showered with gifts and other stuff when I was a kid. But this many years later, those aren't the things that I usually remember or value most.

For example, I couldn't tell you what brand of must-have toy gun Grandma Yeager dutifully bought for all four of her young grandsons for Christmas 1967, although I remember I lost sleep worrying that there wouldn't be one waiting for me under the tree on Christmas morning. Yet I recall like it was just yesterday how the four of us kids used all the **boxes** from the unwrapped Christmas presents to construct something best described as a "Taj Ma Fort Knox Igloo" in Grandma's backyard, a cardboard and snow-covered bastion we attacked and counterattacked for the remainder of that Christmas Day, long after our plastic guns lay broken in the slushy Ohio snow.

And I don't recall any of the store-bought Halloween costumes I wore as a kid. But the one my dad helped me make out of chicken wire, papier-mâché, and an old vacuum cleaner hose will always—for better or worse—be stuck in my memory. It was supposed to be an elephant. Although a few years ago I came across that Halloween headdress carefully preserved in a **dry cleaning bag** in my parents' attic, and I have to say it looked strikingly pornographic.

In his excellent book *Stumbling on Happiness*, author and Harvard College professor of psychology Daniel

Gilbert makes the point that material possessions tend to disappoint us and are forgotten over time, whereas experiences many times stick with us and, if anything, increase in value. Memories appreciate in value while stuff usually depreciates.

The best news is, those experiences or the equipment they involve need not be expensive. Simplicity can be priceless, and oftentimes free.

## Let the Good Times Roll

Here are my favorite ways to have fun with your kids using some commonly thrown away items. Some of them even give you a chance to kick back and relax a bit while your kids amuse themselves.

**Nature Nets:** As kids, when we weren't wearing worn-out **pantyhose** over our heads on Halloween as a cat burglar costume cheapskate-style, we loved to make "nature nets" out of them with **wire coat hangers** to use on our endless butterfly-tadpole-spider-toad hunting expeditions. Just untwist the coat hanger, make it into a loop, and thread the wire through the top of the pantyhose; then twist together the ends of the coat hanger to make a handle. Or stretch just a length of pantyhose over a similar coat hanger hoop, and you have a ready badminton racket for some backyard fun; cut the top off a half-liter **plastic soda bottle** (with the cap on) to use as a shuttlecock.

**Super Soakers:** The first time I managed to save up enough from my weekly allowance to afford a store-bought squirt gun, I remember being royally disappointed. The old dish-washing **soap bottles** and other empty **plastic squeeze bottles** we'd been using up until that time for our water fights had so much more pressure and distance! Of course you want to thoroughly wash out soap, shampoo, and other squeeze bottles before using them as squirt guns, but they work great. Or for DIY plans to make more sophisticated water guns (suitable for adults) out of repurposed items including **plastic soda bottles**, **garden hose**, and **plastic pipe**, check out this website: sscentral.org/homemade/.

**Press Autumn Leaves and Plants:** Use old **phone books** to press interesting leaves and plants collected on nature walks. Just place single leaves between two sheets of repurposed **wax paper** or the **wax paper bag** from inside a **cereal box**, and put them single file between the pages of phone books to press and preserve them (it takes about two weeks for them to fully cure). Better yet, if the kids need a time-out, tell them they have to sit on the phone books to ensure adequate pressure.

**The Marvel of Papier-mâché:** Forget about making quasi-obscene elephant Halloween masks and scale models of Mount Vesuvius for fifth-grade science class. Think BIG when it comes to papier-mâché, as did students from the Salem Lutheran School who broke the world record with a twenty-eight-foot (diameter) globe made out of papier-mâché (see youtube.com/

watch?v=9BjxcFyd9g0). Papier-mâché is not only a great way to repurpose all types of paper—**newspaper**, **phone books**, **copy paper**, **paper bags**, even **magazines** and **cardboard**—but it's easy and cheap to make. The paste is made by heating one part flour to two parts water on the stove for about five minutes, whisking it constantly until it begins to thicken. Better yet, if you have some **stale flour** in the kitchen, it works perfectly in this recipe for papier-mâché paste.

**Put a Cork in It:** Sit down and enjoy a glass of wine while the kids have some fun with the cork. Glue **corks** together to make toy boats, cars, figurines, or other toys—they'll even float. Use a utility knife (careful!) to cut a design in each end of a cork and dip it in ink or paint to use as a personalized stamp. And show your kids one of my favorite *Uncle Jeff Tricks* (similar to *Stupid Pet Tricks*): You can drive a common sewing needle through a penny by first pushing the needle through a cork (lengthways), so that the tip of the needle is barely coming out the other end. Place the point on a penny (on a wooden surface), and hit the opposite end with a hammer. The cork keeps the needle from bending. Remove the cork, and amaze your kids with the mystery of how you drove a needle through a penny. (No corks around the house because, like me, you prefer wine that comes in a box? After you've polished off the box, remove and inflate the **plastic bladder** inside as a beach ball of sorts for the kids.)

**Everybody's a Grown Up Until Somebody Breaks Out the Bubble Wrap:** Sure, **bubble wrap**—particularly the kind with the bigger bubbles—can be folded a few layers thick and put under the cushion of Uncle Jeff's easy chair as a makeshift whoopee cushion. But once the novelty of that gag has worn off, try thumbtacking sheets of unwanted bubble wrap to a worktable and have the kids paint the bubbles with tempera paints. While still wet, press a blank sheet of paper on the painted bubble wrap to make prints of the kid's masterpieces. Use a sponge to keep the paint damp if you want to make a lot of prints. Make designs and even pictures by painting the bubbles different colors, like a giant dot-matrix printer.

**Show School Pride:** Using your school's colors, pour a small amount of tempera paint in a clear **plastic soda bottle**, swirl it around a bit, and let it dry. Add additional colors one at a time, letting each color dry first, until the inside of the bottle is entirely coated. Insert some beans, beads, or similar objects into the bottle to use as a colorful rattle at school pep rallies and games. You can also make your own pompoms out of **plastic shopping bags.** First cut off the handles, then place a stack of them on a flat surface and carefully cut them into strips with a utility knife, leaving about two inches uncut at the bottom of the bag so that the strips remain attached to each other. Roll the stack together, and use tape to secure them and create a handle along the uncut portion at the bottom. The more bags you use, the fluffier your pompoms. They can then be lightly spray painted in your school's colors.

**Not Your Grandma's Tire Swing:** Tire swings have come a long way, baby! When I was a kid, they consisted of an old tire hung from a tree with a rapidly fraying rope (that's why most kids in my neighborhood eventually wound up with steel plates in their heads). The good news is that tire swings are still a great reuse for an old **tire**, and the even better news is that new designs have been developed to make them safer and even more fun. You can find free plans for a sturdy, horizontal-style tire swing in a *Popular Mechanics* article here, popularmechanics.com/home/how-to-plans/backyard-tire-swing-project, and plans for a whimsical "pony tire swing" here, davesgarden.com/files/Pony_Tirc_Swing/.

**Junior Shopkeeper:** One of my favorite pastimes as a kid was tending Yeager's General Store, a corner space in the basement walled off by old **bedsheets** hung from the ceiling. Inside was a store counter and shelves constructed out of **scrap lumber** and **cardboard**. Lining the shelves were empty **cans**, **bottles**, and **boxes** of every grocery item Mom remembered to save rather than throw away so that Yeager's General Store could be properly stocked. I even constructed a cash register out of some of Grandpa's old wooden **cigar boxes** and filled it with **bottle caps**, the only legal tender accepted at my establishment. Man, the hours of fun I had doing business with my friends in that little corner shop, all with items that would otherwise be trash.

**Birdhouses:** What materials do you need to build a birdhouse? A better question is, what materials *can't* you use to build a birdhouse? Few DIY projects allow you to get creative with so many different repurposed materials as does the construction of birdhouses and feeders. Of course birdhouses are a perfect use for **scrap lumber**, but that's only the beginning. What about making a birdhouse/feeder made out of an empty **paint can**, a **plastic soda bottle**, **milk cartons**, emptied out **vacuum cleaner bags**, a leaky **tea kettle**, a hollowed-out **gourd**, or even an old **boot**? Take a look at creative birdhouses made from reclaimed materials at www.trendhunter.com/slideshow/eco-friendly-birdhouse.

*Egg-cellent* **Eggshell Projects:** In Asia, crushed **eggshells** (dyed or natural) are used to make mosaic designs on lacquered objects like decorative boxes and serving trays; bits of shell are simply glued to the object and then covered with multiple coats of clear lacquer. Eggs can also be "blown out" by first thoroughly washing them, then using a needle to prick a small hole in both ends. Blow in one end until the yolk and white is forced out the other end (of course you'll want to save and use the contents of the egg for cooking). The hollowed-out eggs can then be painted and decorated as lasting Easter decorations, or painted with enamel paint and fancifully decorated à la Fabergé. And here's a neat and simple idea: Repurpose bits of **old candles** by carefully melting them down in a double boiler, and then pouring the wax into a partially "decapitated" eggshell (again, dyed or natural); insert a candle wick while the wax is still hot, and you have a conversation-starting tea light candle for the breakfast table. Display your egg candles in soft-boiled egg serving cups or give a dozen as a gift, cleverly packaged in an **egg carton**.

## Work Out in Your Family's Own *Junkyard Gym*

According to the International Health, Racquet & Sportsclub Association (ihrsa.org), U.S. health clubs rake in about $20 billion every year from more than forty-five million members. With most gym memberships costing between $30 to $60 per person, per month (and much more when factoring in commonly charged initiation fees), your family could save a bundle by canceling your memberships and making your own *junkyard gym* instead. Plus, working out and staying fit as a family is more fun.

Consider these fun to make—and fun to use—pieces of exercise equipment for your wastebasket workout.

**Step Aerobics Platform:** Duct tape together old **phone books** or volumes of **yellow pages** to make your own stair-stepper to use in an aerobic workout. The paper is a perfect cushion—so it's soft on your feet—and you can keep adding more and more area codes as your fitness level increases.

**Yoga Training Tool:** Again, old **phone books**—used individually, collectively, or duct taped together—can be helpful in conditioning your body to gradually achieve a variety of those contorted yoga poses you never thought possible. For example, you can master the "Hero Pose"—sitting with your butt on the floor between your feet—by first attempting it with a stack of phone books under your rear (enough to be comfortable). Gradually, over the course of numerous workouts, remove books and even individual pages until your butt makes contact with the floor and you're able to comfortably achieve the meditation pose without needing to call 911.

**Workout Weights:** Try *pumpin' plastic*! Fill different-sized **plastic soda bottles** with water or sand to use as impact-resistant workout weights on land or in the pool. A liter bottle filled with water weighs about 2.2 pounds, and filled with dry sand it's about 2.6 pounds. Workout weights can also be made by similarly filling a variety of plastic containers, particularly those with handles, like **milk jugs** and **laundry detergent bottles**.

**Repurposed Resistance Bands:** Worn-out **pantyhose** with the feet tied together or old **bicycle inner tubes** with the air valve stem cut off make simple elastic bands to use in a variety of resistance training exercises. Working out with resistance bands can not only strengthen and tone muscles, but also increase bone mass and flexibility.

**Medicine Ball**: Save that old **basketball**, **volleyball**, or **soccer ball**—the one with the hole in it—and use a funnel to fill it with sand by removing the air valve or cutting a small incision in it then sealing it with duct tape. Medicine balls are used in a variety of strength and circuit training exercises to enhance their effectiveness.

**Punching and Speed Bags:** A punctured **football** can be unlaced, stuffed with **foam packing peanuts** and relaced, then fastened on a short spring and suspended to use as a homemade speed bag. A variety of worn-out **balls** as well as an old **duffel bag** can be filled with sand (or a mixture of sand and **foam packing peanuts** or **bubble wrap**), hung from the ceiling with a sufficiently strong length of rope or chain, and used as punching bags.

**Barbells:** Barbells and dumbbells in a variety of sizes and weights can be easily made by filling all types of empty plastic or metal containers—**coffee cans**, **plastic nursery pots**, and so on—with a batch of ready-mix mortar or cement, sticking the desired length of old **pipe** into it, and letting it dry (while standing upright). Once one end of the barbell has dried, affix the other end by standing it upright in a matching container of cement/mortar, propping it up as necessary until the concrete cures. Be sure to select a length and type of pipe sufficiently strong to support the amount of weight being used.

**Push-up Handles:** Have an old **clothes iron** (or two) that's beyond repair? If they're sufficiently sturdy, they make perfect push-up handles—exercise devices that you place on the floor and grip when doing push-ups, allowing greater range of motion and building muscle more efficiently. Of course, if you only have one burned out iron, then you'll need to do one-handed push-ups like Rocky Balboa until a second iron bites the dust. Cut off the electrical cord (when it's unplugged, of course), but *Don't Throw That Away!*, because you can use it as a . . .

**Jump Rope:** Old **electrical cords**—like the one you just cut off your burned-out iron or, better yet, the round variety often used on vacuum cleaners—make durable jump ropes. To make a tangle-free jump rope, try this trifecta of repurposing: Save two spent **lint rollers** (the type with the handles and the roll of adhesive paper) and insert the end of an old electrical cord (cut to the desired length) into each handle, securing it with a strong epoxy glue. The handles allow the jump rope to rotate without becoming tangled.

## Deck the Halls with Redux Garbage

Grandma Yeager's specimen-cup Christmas ornaments aside, there really are some terrific ways to decorate for and celebrate the holidays and other special occasions by using repurposed items.

The place to start is with the Holy Trinity when it comes to basic supplies that can be used and reused to decorate for nearly every holiday.

**Wreath Frames:** You can make simple wreath frames by twisting together **wire coat hangers** or **grapevines** or other **vines** found in nature. You can also cut them out of spare **Styrofoam**—maybe some used in packaging or from a Styrofoam ice chest that got crushed. Even if you have to break down and buy a wreath frame—or five—they're inexpensive and so versatile that they'll more than earn their keep. Wreaths are one of those holiday decorations that just keep on giving. Hang colorful hollowed-out **eggs** (see above) on them for Easter; American flags made out of **scrap paper** or **fabric remnants** for President's Day, Flag Day, Veteran's Day, Memorial Day, and the Fourth of July; and other **scrap paper** and **magazine** cutouts for holidays like Valentine's Day, St. Patrick's Day, and Halloween. Add free/cheap natural materials—pine boughs and holly for Christmas, dried leaves and bittersweet for Thanksgiving—and you'll discover that every holiday is wreath-worthy.

**White Twinkle Lights:** I'm hard-pressed to think of a single holiday that wouldn't be brightened by including some simple white twinkle lights in decorating. They can be strung up in different patterns (e.g., egg shaped at Eastertime, a pumpkin design at Halloween, etc.), mixed with different natural materials, incorporated into centerpieces, or even in holiday wreaths (now that you have your wreath frames). And they don't always need to *appear* white: string a few in colored **plastic or glass bottles**, or in luminaries made with colored **scrap paper or paper bags**, or behind a screen of repurposed colored **tissue paper** or thin **wrapping paper** for a stained-glass effect. Try stringing them against a backdrop of repurposed **aluminum foil**, or through the holes in unwanted **CDs/DVDs** to create a super-reflective light show.

**A Star Is Born:** Besides all being holidays, what do New Year's, President's Day, Memorial Day, Flag Day, Independence Day, Veteran's Day, Hanukkah, and Christmas all have in common? Answer: They're all holidays when stars are commonly used in decorations and celebrations. You can't have too many stars stockpiled along with your other holiday decorating supplies. And there are as many ways to make stars out of repurposed materials as there are—you guessed it—stars in the sky. Cut them out of unwanted **cardboard** and cover them in repurposed **aluminum foil**, **wrapping paper**, or even pretty pictures from **magazines**. Use **scrap paper** to make fancy origami stars, or if that's too complicated, try this nifty trick at ushistory.org/betsy/flagstar.html for making a perfect star with a single snip of the scissors. Three-dimensional stars can be made by folding, cutting, and pasting together old **greeting cards**, or by cutting the corners off one **cardboard box** and gluing them to the sides of a second square box, then painting or "gift wrapping" it to look pretty. It's also easy to make cool stars out of pieces of **aluminum cans**; just cut out the shapes with sturdy scissors (careful, the edges are sharp!) and then crimp them slightly with a pair of pliers.

## Shocking Eco Facts

Comedian Henny Youngman was on to something when he said, "I know a man who doesn't pay to have his trash collected. How does he get rid of his trash? He gift wraps it, and puts it into an unlocked car." The irony is, most of the $2.9 billion in **gift wrap paper** and supplies sold in the United States each year (per Hallmark) ends up being thrown away, which is one of the reasons why between Thanksgiving and New Year's we generate an extra million tons of waste *each week*, according to the California Department of Resources Recycling and Recovery. That includes thirty-eight thousand miles of **ribbon**, enough to stretch from New York to California more than a dozen times. Then of course there are the 2.6 billion **holiday cards** we buy each year, enough to fill a football field ten stories high.

## Rapping About Wrapping and Such

Now that you know the true cost of holiday gift wrapping and decorating, let's save a couple bucks—or a couple BILLION bucks—by being a bit smarter and more creative about it, shall we?

Of course wrapping paper can simply be saved, put back on the roll, and used again. In fact, my great-aunt had some Christmas gift wrap that dated back to B.C., if that's possible. Wrapping kids' gifts in the colorful Sunday comics from the **newspaper** is a classic alternative, as is using an old **map** to wrap a travel-related gift. Wrapping gifts in brown **paper bags** provides the perfect canvas for then decorating them yourself with drawings, stencils, paints, stamps, or pretty scenes cut and pasted from old **greeting cards** or **magazines**. You can even attractively wrap gifts in those obnoxious **plastic shopping bags** by lightly spray painting them for a sort of metallic look.

If you save your wrapping paper or just have some extra, store rolls of gift wrap paper in old **pantyhose**—one roll per leg—and hang them over a **coat hanger** in the closet to keep paper neat and tatter-free. One of my Miser Advisers also says storing rolls of gift wrap in an old **garment bag**—again hung in the closet—keeps things neat and convenient.

If you're looking for a way to store those pesky **foam packing peanuts** that magically seem to fly all over the house whenever you open a box from UPS, store them in—you guessed it!—an old pair of **pantyhose** as well. Snip a small hole in the toe and keep it tied off with a **twisty seal** so that you can conveniently dispense the peanuts next time you pack a gift box. And for storing small or fragile Christmas tree ornaments or other holiday decorations that might get misplaced or damaged, nothing works better than cardboard or Styrofoam **egg cartons**.

**Greeting cards** for all occasions can easily be repurposed (much to Hallmark's chagrin). Cut and paste the pretty picture and message on blank card stock to make a "new card," or go the more direct route, as we prefer at the House of Cheap: My wife and I have been exchanging the same two birthday cards with each other for more than twenty years. Not only has it saved us a lot of money, but it also keeps me feeling young. The card she's still giving me reads, "Happy 30th Birthday to My Dear Husband."

## More Nifty-Thrifty Repurposing Tips for Holiday Fun

**Groundhog Day:** Maybe it's not a major holiday, but it's a perfect chance to repurpose old **socks**—or a sock without a mate—by making groundhog hand puppets or stuffed groundhog decorations. If the socks aren't already a shade becoming a proper groundhog, dye them and then add **buttons** for eyes and use **fabric remnants** for whiskers, paws, and so on.

**All-Natural Easter Eggs:** For organic Easter egg dye, just boil your eggs with some **onion skins**. You'll end up with wild, Grateful-Dead-ish yellow and orange eggshells, all without the use of artificial dyes.

**Extra Christmas Sparkle:** Unwanted **CDs and DVDs** hung with colorful bits of leftover **ribbon** or **yarn** are a great way to decorate large outdoor trees for Christmas. They sparkle in the sunlight, and if you have colored lights on the tree, they create a rainbow of reflections when the lights come on at night.

**New Year's Eve *Espana* Style:** I picked up this one a few years ago when we spent New Year's Eve in Spain, where this repurposing practice is very common and festive. Save colorful foil-type **gift wrapping paper** from Christmas or used **aluminum foil** and wrap an empty two-liter **plastic soda bottle** in it like a giant piece of hard candy, twisting off both ends and fastening with leftover strands of colorful **ribbon.** Hang several of them together—inside or out—like bunches of huge firecrackers ready to end the year with a bang.

## Guess She Won't Be Giving Up Lint for Lent

Maybe it was heavenly inspiration. Or maybe it was just laundry fatigue.

Laura Bell of Roscommon, Michigan, is convinced her rapid ascension from home health aide to fine artist was the former. Laura's very first work of art sold for $12,000, although it did take her an estimated two hundred hours to make. And that's not including the full year she spent doing laundry in order to amass the necessary art supplies.

You see, Laura doesn't work in oils, or watercolors, or even clay. Laura's chosen medium is **dryer lint**. "My dryer is my palette," she told me with genuine Midwestern sincerity in an interview. It all started in 2008 when Laura removed a load of wash from the family's dryer and went to clean the lint trap. "I remember that it was a beautiful teal blue. And I thought, it's a shame to throw this away. I can do something with this," she said. A devoted Christian, Laura adds, "I really think it was a revelation. The idea (of using lint in art) just came to me."

As Laura began to experiment with using dryer lint to make painting-like, two-dimensional wall hangings, she quickly discovered that all dryer lint is not created equal. In order to get the definition and textures she wanted in her work, she needed to dry specific types and colors of fabrics.

Unfortunately, Laura has found that expensive new towels provide some of the best lint for her projects, so she's been buying and drying a lot of them. A whole lot of them, since some of Laura's most impressive masterpieces are impressive in size as well. Her rendering of the Last Supper—the piece that sold to Ripley's Believe It or Not for $12,000—measures four feet by fourteen feet, and her recent portrait of Adam and Eve was even larger.

Without any training or prior experience in the arts (although she has done a lot of laundry over the years), Laura has developed her own techniques for working with dryer lint. First she makes a rough sketch—almost like a "paint by numbers" outline—on the corrugated plastic sheeting that is her canvas. She then uses spray glue to apply the first layer of lint to the background.

"The good thing is, lint sticks to lint, so the other

layers (sometimes as many as *five* other layers) don't usually need to be glued," she explained about how she manages to get the eye-catching depth and texture in her pieces.

Given the size of her masterpieces, I asked Laura about her studio. "Oh, no, I don't have one. I just work on my kitchen table. It's really getting a little out of control," she admits.

And what are the downsides of her newfound artistic expression? "Well, the cat likes to claw the lint off my pictures if I leave them in the hallway to dry," she said with a sigh. As they say, "One must sacrifice for one's art."

# Chapter 6
## Clothing and Fabric

**Answer:** *I cut it in half and made a blouse out of the top and a skirt out of the bottom . . . plus a couple of dozen sachet packets to give as gifts. I knew I'd never wear the whole thing again. Right, Jeffrey?*
Denise Y. (as in "Yeager"—a.k.a. "My Pooooor Wife"—Accokeek, Maryland)

**Question:** *What can you do with your old **wedding dress**?*

There are many reasons why I love my wife—her sense of humor, kind heart, and ability to put up with me, all among them. But when shortly after our wedding Denise confidently chopped her beautiful ivory-colored wedding dress in two, I knew for sure that I'd married my true soul mate.

Before our wedding, she'd proudly bragged to friends and family about how little she'd paid for her wedding dress. "Less than any bridesmaid dress I've ever had to buy to be in someone else's wedding!" she loved telling people. It occurred to me at the time that most brides-to-be would likely brag about just the opposite: how *much* their wedding dress cost, not how *little*. But that's the woman I married, thankfully, almost thirty years ago.

I also knew that Denise would be a perfect fit with my extended, rather quirky family. Not just because of her inescapable charm—or a pronounced frugal streak of her own (a virtue admired by all Yeagers)—but, specifically, because of Denise's passion for needlecraft. My mother and both of my grandmothers loved to sew, knit, crochet, quilt, and even dabble in weaving, so I knew my bride was going to fit in like a thread through a needle.

As you might guess, while the seamstresses of the Yeager clan love a bolt of fresh fabric as much as any sewing enthusiast, they revel even more in the challenge and sense of accomplishment that comes from repurposing material they already have.

We're talking about unraveling old **sweaters** and re-using the yarn to knit something new. We're talking about saving swatches of fabric from everything from worn-out **shirts** to old dish **towels** and transforming them into keepsake quilts. We're talking about making skirts and vests out of old **neckties**; handbags out of faded **blue jeans**; and crocheted hats out of beer or other **aluminum cans** (see rrrhi5.com/uploads/CanHat.pdf). And, yes, we're talking about having the self-confidence (and the pinking shears) to amputate your own wedding dress at the waist, all in the name of creative repurposing.

## The Coming Change of Clothing?

Prepare for shock and awe: According to the Natural Resources Defense Council (NRDC.org), the average American now throws away sixty-eight POUNDS of clothing every year! Only a small percentage of that apparel is truly "worn out" in the sense that it's threadbare, torn, or horribly stained. The vast majority of the clothing we throw away is just stuff we've grown tired of, outgrown, or is "so last year's fashion" we can't imagine ever wearing it again.

Of course, the simple alternative is to sell or donate unwanted apparel to someone who can use it (see Chapter 8). But there's increasing interest—literally a "rebellion"—brewing when it comes to restitching, opposed to just ditching, unwanted clothing.

The group Sewing Rebellion, for example, hosts free workshops and is attempting to create local chapters to teach people how to alter, mend, and make their own garments. They hope to "emancipate people from the global garment industry," or as their official motto asserts, "Stop Shopping Start Sewing." Their website (sewingrebellion.wordpress.com) offers a number of free patterns and instructions for DIY projects, including a "trouser makeover" and a "table cloth circle skirt."

Jenny Allen of Port Townsend, Washington, has been at the forefront of what she calls the "refashioning movement." Jenny is a full-time refashionista and owner of Jenny Jo Clothing (jennyjoclothing.com), a small but rapidly growing enterprise devoted entirely to "found fashion"—transforming old clothing into entirely new garments.

For Jenny, "it all started with a shrunken sweater," she likes to say. In 2007, shortly before her daughter Flora was born, Jenny pondered over what to do with one of her own sweaters that had shrunken like a frightened turtle. She got creative and refashioned it into a darling little sweater dress for her daughter to one day wear.

Jenny views refashioning as part of a broader *domestic renaissance*, which she sees as driven in large part by the recession. "Many people now have more time than they have money," she told me, "so we're rediscovering a lot of skills and practices like sewing . . . things that have really become lost arts."

"It (the refashioning phenomenon) is growing incredibly fast," Jenny says. "Some major retail chains are now starting to carry lines of new clothing that are made to look like they're refashioned out of old garments!" Jenny's creations—ranging from gloves and hats made from old **sweaters** to "tee-skirts" made from, you guessed it, old **T-shirts**—are made from 100 percent repurposed garments, although she does use new thread and elastic in her clothing makeovers. Most of the garments she uses in her refashioning come from thrift stores, including many that would likely end up in the landfill, since she's often able to work around stains and other flaws that reduce a garment's resale appeal.

"People are always saying how creative my clothing is," she says, "but I tell them that it's just the kind of thing our grandmothers did all the time." All you Grandma Yeagers, take a bow.

## Duds Redux

Here are a few refashioning projects to whet your bobbin, from simple and practical to interesting and, well, unique.

**Simple T-Shirt Transformations:** Jenny Allen's advice is to dive right in to the new world of old clothes remodeling, even if you're just a novice with needle and thread. Two starter projects she recommends involve repurposing old T-shirts. The first is making a **superhero kid's cape,** which involves no sewing whatsoever. Simply cut the sleeves off an adult-sized T-shirt at an angle, then continue cutting down both sides all the way to the bottom. Go back and cut around the front of the collar, so it remains intact and attached to the back of the shirt (in other words, you have removed the front of the shirt at this point). Trim it further to resemble a fan shape, if desired. Jenny's second starter project is making a **simple "tee-skirt"** from an old T-shirt. It's as easy as cutting off a T-shirt below the armpits (to the desired length), and then adding an elastic waistband along that seam. The bottom hem of the T-shirt becomes the bottom hem of the skirt. How's that for simple?

**Blue Jean Basics:** *The durability of denim knows no limits.* Little wonder it's the fabric that built the jeans that built America. Sure, when the knees get worn out, cut off your jeans to make shorts. But never ever throw away the legs or any other piece of denim —that's a mortal sin among creative repurposers. The legs and other spare parts can be used to make everything from purses, pouches, and wine bags, to coverings for books, pillows, and picture frames. Denim is a popular and versatile fabric for reusing in the type of weaving and braiding applications described below, as well as in quilting and even upholstery. And while any and all worn-out fabric is rag-worthy, a denim rag is the ultimate, indestructible cleaning rag.

**Retread Sandals:** I came across this one on a bicycle trip in Mexico back in the 1980s. The tread from old **car tires** makes a durable—and a fairly comfortable—sole for homemade sandals. Use chalk to trace an outline of both feet on the tread of a nonradial tire. Cutting the rubber takes some muscle and persistence; I've found that a reciprocating saw with a bimetal blade works best. Once you've cut out the soles, make straps to hold them on your feet from an old **leather belt**, a **bicycle inner tube**, or similar material. Fit one strap over the crown of your foot and a second strap around the back of your ankle so your foot is firmly held in place. Use screws (drywall screws work well) to fasten the straps to the side of the soles. I then add a strip of trim (either **bicycle inner tube** or old **garden hose** . . . for a real fashion statement) around the entire edge of each sandal, again fastening it to the soles with screws. Now that's one roadworthy pair of sandals.

**Stretching Your Undergarments, So to Speak:** I credit my wife with this tip, but she insists that other frugal women pioneered the practice long before her. In a pinch, Denise has been known to double up on her **pantyhose**: If she has a run in the left leg and a matching pair with a run in the right, she'll cut off the bad legs and double up, wearing two layers of panty tops with a good leg attached to each. Also, always save the hook and strap portions from worn-out **bras** to use as "bra extenders" in the future, sewing them on to retrofit bras that have become a little too snug.

**Hanger T-Tote:** And here's an Ultimate Cheapskate original design (as far as I know). It's simple to make—I didn't even need Denise's help—and it repurposes both an old **T-shirt** and two of those overpopulated **plastic clothes hangers** (only 7,998,000,000 to go—see below). Just fold the top of a T-shirt to seal off the openings for the neck and the arms, and then stitch a couple of heavy seam across the length of that fold to form the bottom of the bag. Take two plastic coat hangers, with hooks facing in opposite directions to form the handle of the bag, and attach them to the top of the bag by stitching them under a fold of fabric along the bottom/waist of the shirt.

## Shocking Eco Facts

It's one of those things you never really think about, but when you do a little research into it, what you find is pretty unbelievable. According to the environmental news website Green Progress (greenprogress.com), over eight billion plastic and wire clothes hangers are sold in the United States each year, mostly with new apparel. By their calculations, that's enough to fill all 102 floors of the Empire State Building . . . more than four times over. Surprisingly, only about 15 percent of all hangers are recycled. Even most of those hangers you don't take home with you from the store are thrown away at the end of the day. Why aren't more hangers recycled? In part because wire hangers tend to foul up recycling machinery, so many recycling programs won't accept them. And plastic hangers can be made of several different types of plastics, each needing to be identified and processed separately by recyclers. So most hangers end up in the landfill, where the plastic ones take about a thousand years to decompose. Try giving away unwanted hangers on websites like freecycle.org and Craigslist, donating them to thrift stores, or—in the case of wire hangers—asking your local dry cleaner if they'll reuse them.

## Better Clothing Care through Creative Repurposing

**Shoe and Leather Care:** Showing your shoes and boots a little TLC can more than double their expected life span, according to a shoe repairman I met a few years ago. Among other footwear factoids and tips he shared with me are the following:

- Moisture—from both perspiration and inclement weather—is actually harder on leather footwear than daily wear and tear. He suggests never wearing the same pair of shoes two days in a row, giving them a day off to dry out. He also suggests stuffing crumpled-up **newspaper** in your shoes every night when you take them off to help wick up moisture.

- A briquette of **charcoal** or two stuffed inside an old **sock** and placed inside each shoe will also absorb both moisture and odor. Make shoes smell even sweeter by adding a couple of old **fabric softener sheets**, too.

- To help boots and shoes retain their shape during storage, try stuffing them with crumpled-up **aluminum foil**, **plastic soda bottles**, or **foam packing peanuts**.

- When it comes to polishing shoes and boots, buffing them with a length of old **pantyhose** really makes them shine, as will polishing them with spent **fabric softener sheets**. And here's one that sounds weird but really works: Try polishing your shoes with the slippery side

of a **banana peel** then buffing them down . . .
I call it a "banana split shine."

**Laundry and Fabric Care:** Laundering is tough on fabrics, and these days we've gone laundry crazy compared to earlier times. Consider washing your clothes and other textile items less often, and wash only in cold water whenever possible. Drying garments on an old-fashioned clothesline (repurposed **electrical cord** makes a good one) can extend the life of your clothing exponentially compared to using an electric or gas dryer. Here are some other ideas for reusing items to extend the life of your precious clothing:

- Keep a couple used **disposable razors** handy in your clothes closets and dressers to shave off those fuzzy balls of nap that develop on wool and other fabrics.

- Use old **pantyhose** like a mitten to remove pet hair and lint from clothing and upholstery rather than using a lint brush. It will also remove deodorant residue from clothing.

- You can literally *foil* static cling by putting a crumpled-up piece of used **aluminum foil** in the dryer with your clothing. It magically reduces static electricity. Who knew?

- Put used **dryer sheets** in with sweaters and other seasonal clothing before you store them. It'll not only make them smell fresher, but the smell helps keep mice away.

- Another trifecta of repurposed items provides an eco-friendly alternative to toxic mothballs for protecting stored clothing from insect damage: Combine pieces of dried **lemon rinds** with **cedar sawdust** (**pencil shavings** from a cedar pencil will work, too) in—what else—a length of old **pantyhose.**

## What Can't You Use to Make Fabric?

Silk, cotton, wool, nylon: All are among the most commonly used materials for manufacturing textiles. But creative repurposers with an interest in making their own fabric need look no further than their own trash for all the raw materials they need. Whether by weaving, knitting, crocheting, braiding, knotting, or some other fabric-making method, here are some materials you can use to make trash into textiles.

**Plastic Shopping Bags**: Making the best of an environmentally disastrous product, creative repurposers have developed an ingenious DIY method for transforming those ubiquitous plastic shopping bags into what they call "plarn"—a "plastic yarn" to use in making fabric. Bags are folded, cut into strips, and twisted, and then used in weaving, knitting, and so on. The method for making plarn is simple enough, although hard to explain in words, but this short video shows you how: youtube.com/watch?v=dj1pVVjtqRk. Plarn is what one of my Miser Advisers used to crochet the clever shopping bag I mentioned in Chapter 1. You can find a similar pattern at etsy.com/blog/en/2010/how-tuesday-how-to-make-plarn-crochet-an-eco-friendly-tote-b/.

**Bread Wrappers:** Long before the invention of "plarn," Grandma Yeager was saving plastic bread bags and using them to make small braided rugs and doormats. Since they're waterproof and quite durable, she used them as welcome mats at the doors to the outside and as bathmats. Similar in technique to making braided rugs from rags and other cloth materials, lengths of plastic roping are made by twisting bags together (the mouth of one slightly overlapping the bottom of the next, and so on). Three ropes are then braided together into a single flat strand and stitched off at the ends to keep it from unraveling. The braided strand is then simply coiled flat, round and round itself to the desired size, and then the coils are stitched together with fishing line or heavy thread. A similar technique can be used for braiding rugs out of any type of **plastic bag**, including shopping bags or those very sheer plastic bags you get in the produce department at the supermarket.

**Cloth Rags:** And long before there was either plarn *or* bread wrappers, for centuries people recycled all types of previously used textiles into new fabric and other products. "Rag and bone men" in England—and their counterparts in many other regions of the world—would travel door-to-door collecting rags to be used in making new fabric or paper, and bones to be used for making glue and buttons. Some rags were literally unraveled and the thread used to weave new fabric, à la Grandma Yeager and her reused yarn. Short of that approach, all types of textiles—leftover **fabric**

remnants, **old clothing**, **towels**, **bed linens**, **draperies**, even **T-shirts**—can simply be cut into strips and used to make new fabric via most traditional textile-making methods (i.e., weaving, knitting, crocheting, etc.). Strips of rags can also be braided together to make items like rag rugs and placements, using the same basic process described for bread wrapper rugs.

**Newspaper:** Perhaps more of a novelty than a material for making durable, versatile fabric, newsprint can fairly easily be cut into strips and then twisted together to form a rough paper cord for use in weaving things like floor mats, wall hangings, and baskets. Read more about it at greenupgrader.com/2138/handspun-recycled-newspaper-yarn/.

**And You Won't Believe What Else:** Although not really do-it-yourself projects, it's good to know that textile manufacturers are also climbing on the repurposing bandwagon. Some of the more unusual would-be trash used to manufacture fabric today includes **plastic bottles**, **old CDs and DVDs**, **wood pulp**, **coffee and tea grounds**, milk protein casein, nettles, and bamboo.

But those alternative textile materials are far from best of show. Texas-based VIP Fibers specializes in spinning your **pet's spare hair** into yarn for your favorite knitting or weaving project. Or you can read up on how to do the same thing yourself, with a book by Kendall

Crolius and Anne Montgomery that just may have the best title of any book ever: *Knitting with Dog Hair: Better a Sweater from a Dog You Know and Love Than from a Sheep You'll Never Meet.*

# Chapter 7
## Garden and Yard

**Answer:** *I tie them all together and keep them soaking in a sprinkling can full of water. It's an easy way to give my plants a quick drink of nitrogen.*
Sally B. (Yellow Springs, Ohio)

**Question:** *What can you do with spent **teabags**?*

I love what I call the *soil sports*—gardening, landscaping, and anything that gets me outside and my hands really dirty. Soil sports are a perfect example of an enjoyable hobby that can not only save you money, but also keep you fit and maybe even *make* you some money if you do it right.

By doing more things for yourself—like mowing the lawn, raking leaves, or tending your own flower beds—you can save some serious green compared to the cost of hiring someone to do those simple tasks for you. You'll also be surprised how much you can trim your grocery bill by planting a small backyard vegetable garden, or even sticking a few veggie plants or herbs in among your flower beds or in a container on the back porch.

And landscaping can dramatically increase both the value and energy efficiency of your home. A Michigan State University study found that landscaping can add 5 to 11 percent to the value of a home (depending on the location of the home and type of landscaping), making it one of the most cost-effective of all home improvements. What's more, according to the American Public Power Association (publicpower.org), landscaping can reduce air-conditioning costs by up to 50 percent by shading the windows, walls, and roof of your home. Now that's what I call a growing investment—or an investment worth growing.

But of course landscaping, gardening, and other yard care can also be expensive. The National Gardening Association (garden.org) estimates retail sales of lawn and garden products to U.S. consumers at nearly $40 billion annually, with the average American household spending roughly $500 each year on do-it-yourself lawn and garden activities. Note that both of those figures only include the cost of garden products and supplies, not what we spend on lawn and garden services and labor. Add those costs in and annual spending on our yards more than doubles.

Is it possible to play major-league *soil sports* on a farm team budget? Is there a way to get more begonias for your buck, so to speak? Sure, since you're probably already throwing away lots of stuff that can be reused in the yard and garden. Best of all, these repurposing tips for the yard and garden are ultra-eco-friendly, too.

## Cultivating Healthier Plants

Blue-ribbon-worthy plants depend on soil packed with all the essential life-giving nutrients. Look no further than your trash can for a plethora of environmentally sound ingredients for enriching garden soil and raising healthier plants.

Of course compost is king when it comes to repurposing all types of **organic material** and transforming it into rich humus that can then be tilled in to improve any soil. Properly prepared compost not only boosts the nutrients in soil that plants crave, but it improves the soil's structure, promoting better root growth and helping to retain moisture so that you can water less often.

Aside from composting—which I discuss every rotten detail of in the next chapter—here are some would-be throwaways that can be worked directly into the soil to increase essential nutrients:

- **Banana peels** are rich in potassium and can be chopped up and stirred directly into the soil. Your potassium-craving rose bushes will find them especially "apeeling," particularly since banana peels also help to deter aphids, which love your rose bushes as much as you do.

- **Charcoal**—either leftover briquettes or the remnants of barbecues gone by from the bottom of the grill—can be pulverized with a hammer and added in small amounts to the soil to increase carbon and alkalinity and to promote better drainage. Some indoor plants, including orchids and bromeliads, thrive in soil enhanced with a small amount of charcoal too.

- **Coffee grounds**—as well as the tea from spent **teabags**—will boost nitrogen, and scattering them on the surface of the soil will help deflect a variety of garden pests.

- **Wood ashes** from the fireplace are a good solution if your soil has a low pH level, since they're typically composed of about 25 percent calcium carbonate, a common liming material used to increase soil alkalinity. They also contain smaller amounts of potash, phosphate, iron, boron, zinc, copper, and manganese, all important plant nutrients. Ashes can also be applied directly to lawns to boost pH levels, but go easy on it and always test your soil first. Otherwise you might increase soil alkalinity too much, and that could be a real pain in the ash.

- **Rotten meat**, **fish carcasses**, **spoiled dairy products**, and, yes, even **roadkill** are given a proper burial by some hard-core horticulturalists in their backyard gardens. While most experts advise against putting meat or dairy products in your compost pile for fear of attracting vermin and creating an odor capable of inspiring a neighborhood uprising, burying animal protein under a layer of at least twelve to eighteen inches of soil allows it to safely decompose and release nitrogen, carbon, and other beneficial nutrients.

- **Animal bones** can also be dried and then pulverized into bone meal, a popular organic product for increasing phosphorous and calcium in garden soil.

Mulch is also an invaluable asset in the yard and garden. It both inhibits unwanted weed growth and, like compost, helps to retain moisture. Particularly in the lawn-crazed U.S. (80% of Americans have a lawn, with the average size being one-third acre!), we could save a lot of money on water, fertilizers, herbicides, and pesticides if we reduced the size of our lawns by planting low-maintenance ground covers or mulching over parts of our yards.

You can often score free mulch by chatting it up with highway crews clearing **brush and trees** along area roadsides since they're usually happy to find a convenient spot to dump their load of chips. Many public landfills also pulverize **scrap lumber** and other **wood products** they receive onsite and then offer the resulting mulch to local citizens at bargain prices.

Particularly if you have a lot of **yard debris**, such as downed **tree branches** and **trees**, **underbrush**, **leaves**, and other **woody plant material**, investing in an electric or gas-powered "chipper-shredder" may make sense. These pulverizing machines—made infamous in the movie *Fargo*—allow you to quickly turn organic material (preferably *not* the type of organic material shredded in *Fargo*) into coarse-grade mulch. The downside is that the most useful, heavier-duty chipper-shredders can easily cost $1,000+.

Regardless of how you come by your mulch, put down a few layers of **newspaper**, **phone book pages**, uncoated **scrap paper**, or even a layer or two of **cardboard** first, and then spread the mulch on top. This acts as a perfect biodegradable weed blocker and works with the mulch to retain even more moisture. Call me a *garden fashionista*, but I love this layered look when it comes to my mulch.

In addition to giving plants optimum soil conditions to promote growth, it's important to start them out right in life. When starting plants indoors from seeds before the weather is warm enough for them to be transplanted outside, instead of using commercial peat pots, try filling any of the following with light potting soil to make perfect little seed-starter containers:

- **eggshell halves**, which also provide calcium to the plants and soil;
- **cardboard toilet paper** and **paper towel tubes** (cut into one-inch lengths and set on a plate);
- scooped-out **avocado shells**;
- **cardboard egg cartons**.

All these seed starters are biodegradable, so they can be crumbled up and stirred into the soil once the seedlings are ready to transplant outside.

Young plants require a little extra lovin' as they stake their claim and literally put down roots in the garden. Protect tender stems of seedlings (particularly tomato plants) from insect damage with a loose-fitting collar made of repurposed **newspaper**, **phone book** pages, or **aluminum foil**, extending about half an inch under the soil and an inch or so above. Paper collars will decompose naturally, but foil collars should be removed as the plants mature.

Some repurpose-oriented gardeners also swear by removing both ends of **tin or aluminum cans** and using them as season-long collars around plants like peppers and tomatoes. They claim it not only wards off pests but also helps to trap and direct water to the plant's roots throughout the growing season. You might say those gardeners have a "can do" attitude.

When it's time to stake up tall tender-stemmed plants like tomatoes and peppers, or flowers like peonies or sunflowers, cut old **pantyhose** into strips for plant ties with just the right amount of elasticity. Tie snugly but loose enough for stems and vines to grow.

Given the multitude of tips for reusing old **pantyhose** in the garden and elsewhere, you're probably thinking to yourself, *Jeff, just how many pairs of pantyhose does a guy like you wear out in a year?* Miser Adviser and gardening guru Paul Swearingen of Topeka, Kansas, gets asked the same question a lot: "If you personally don't wear panty hose, consider visiting the nearest retirement home with some of your surplus garden truck and ask the administrator to put out a container for panty hose disposal . . . ankle hose are fine, too. I find that little old ladies love prepared horseradish, for example—the more unusual the item, the better chance you have of trading for old hosiery!" Cash for Clunkers/Horseradish for Hosiery, I guess.

### Shocking Eco Facts

According to the nonprofit organization Beyond Pesticides (BeyondPesticides.org), "of 30 commonly used lawn pesticides, 19 have studies pointing toward carcinogens, 13 are linked with birth defects, 21 with reproductive effects, 15 with neurotoxicity, 26 with liver or kidney damage, 27 are sensitizers and/or irritants, and 11 have the potential to disrupt the endocrine (hormonal) system." In related news: The EPA (EPA.gov) reports that 78 million U.S. households use home and garden pesticides each year, with sales of chemical pesticides now topping $9 billion annually. I guess poisoning yourself ain't cheap.

### Controlling Garden Pests

Did you know that garden slugs can regrow their heads, are hermaphroditic (having both male and female sex organs), and they love beer? Plant-ravaging garden slugs will at least die happy—although still sexually confused—if you bury a shallow **plastic container**, leftover **aluminum pie plate**, or half of a **Styrofoam or plastic "clamshell"** up to its lip in soil and put a little **stale beer** in it. Slugs will crawl in for a drink . . . and it'll be their last.

You can also deter slugs, snails, and cutworms by scattering crushed **eggshells** or **nutshells** around your plants and flowers since those creepy crawlers are turned off by the rough texture and make a U-turn as soon as they encounter them.

Speaking of **eggshells**, deer hate the smell of eggs, so placing a few around deer-tempting plants will help keep them at bay. Even more effective, if you ever find yourself with some truly "**rotten eggs**," mix them thoroughly with water and sprinkle the foul-smelling concoction around plants you want to protect. Other repurposing tips for deterring deer include sprinkling **human or pet hair** around plants, or leftover **slivers of soap** (the stronger smelling, the better). Also try hanging strands of **aluminum foil** or lengths of old **plastic video or audiotape** on the low-hanging branches of trees and other plants.

And if all else fails, *pee may be the key*. **Urine**—your own or your pet's—will help to repel deer. Just make sure you don't apply it directly to the plants you're trying to protect; instead, create a tinkle barrier a few feet away.

Old-fashioned scarecrows are not only a cool garden accoutrement, they really do work in keeping away birds, deer, and other animals, as well some knock-kneed teens who might otherwise be tempted to raid your garden on a stormy night. Building a scarecrow is an opportunity for master repurposers to prove their mettle. Sure, start with a frame made of **scrap lumber**, leftover **wire** and **fencing**, and old **clothing** from everybody's closets. But go the extra mile: use **plastic bags** filled with **foam packing peanuts** instead of traditional straw stuffing; incorporate old **bedsheets**, **draperies**, and other **fabric remnants** as much as possible (the more flowing the costume, the more effective it will be in scaring off pests); and make yours a high-tech scarecrow by covering him with unwanted **CDs and DVDs** (shiny side out) to really keep away the critters. Gardeners swear that the reflection of the sun off the CDs/DVDs is the biggest breakthrough in scarecrow technology since the *Wizard of Oz*.

In the garden or home, trap flying insects and some that crawl with a simple trap made out of a two-liter plastic **soda bottle**. Just cut the top third off the bottle, and then invert it like a funnel into the bottom portion. Put a little **rotten fruit**, leftover **juice**, or sugar water in the bottom as bug bait. Insects will dive in, but they won't be able to get back out.

So a guy walks into a dentist's office and says, "Doc, you've gotta help me! I think I'm turning into a moth!" The dentist says, "Sir, you really need to see a psychiatrist. I'm a dentist." The guy says, "Yeah, I know. But your light was on." Moral to that bad joke: Inside and outside the home, hanging a spent **fabric softener sheet** in front of lightbulbs and lighting fixtures will help to keep moths, mosquitoes, and other flying insects from gravitating to the light.

And finally: "Is that a zucchini in your **pantyhose**, or are you just happy to see me?" Yep, that's right. Once again it's worn-out pantyhose to the rescue. Slip a length of pantyhose over your prized veggies and fruits while they're still growing on the plant in order to keep insects, birds, and other pests from attacking them.

## A Few Words About Weeds

Controlling unwanted weeds in the garden and around your yard need not involve expensive—and environmentally harmful—chemical herbicides. A number of commonly thrown away items can be employed to effectively help kill and control weeds:

- **Vinegar**—even what's leftover after the last gherkin has left the jar or the last pickled beet has beat it—can be poured directly on unwanted weeds to wipe them out. This works particularly well on weeds with deep tap roots, like dandelions, curly dock, chicory, and plantain. (Of course, since all four of those types of weeds are edible, you might just want to pull them instead and use the pickle vinegar to dress them as a dinner salad.)

- Think twice before dumping the **boiling water** from that pot of pasta or potatoes down the sink. I like to carry the pot directly to the backyard and drain the scalding water on unwanted weeds. I find boiling water is especially effective when it comes to killing weeds that have taken root in the cracks in the patio and driveway, or larger patches of leafier weeds.

- Ever wonder what to do with that leftover **rock salt** after the last snows of winter have melted? Rock salt—or any type of **salt**, for that matter—can be used to kill weeds and keep new weeds from sprouting up. In fact, I stock up on rock salt at the end of the winter season, when it's usually deeply discounted, to use for weed control during the growing season. It's particularly convenient for sprinkling on gravel pathways and gravel driveways to keep weeds at bay. Salt also makes a good weed barrier along lawn edgings and other places you can't reach with a lawn mower. But apply it carefully, since salt will erode concrete surfaces and can leave the ground barren for a protracted period of time.

- Low-growing weeds like clover and crabgrass can be killed by simply covering them for a couple of weeks with several layers of **newspaper**, **fabric remnants** (including **carpet remnants**), or opaque **plastic bags/sheeting**—anything that will cut off their supply of sunlight.

## Gardening Tools and Equipment

Keep shovels, hoes, pruning shears, and other garden tools from rusting by storing their "business ends" in a bucket full of sand saturated with used **motor oil**. You can also keep tools rust-free by storing them wrapped in a garbage bag with a few pieces of leftover **charcoal** in it. This charcoal trick also works well for winterizing your lawnmower and keeping chainsaws rust-free.

Used **aluminum foil** makes a very effective scrub pad for removing grime and rust from garden tools if it does develop. Aluminum foil can also be used to sharpen pruning and other gardening shears simply by folding it several layers thick and then cutting through it a few times.

Do your knees and back kill you when you garden? Outdated **phone books** wrapped shut with duct tape make a comfortable kneeling pad when you're weeding garden beds.

I like to wrap the handles of my garden rakes, hoes, and other hand tools with old **bicycle inner tubes**, secured with duct tape, to make for a more comfortable, slip-resistant grip. Many bike shops will give you old inner tubes from their repair jobs if you just ask.

For garden and landscape irrigation, simple "slow leak" watering devices can be made out of two-liter **plastic bottles** by puncturing the bottoms slightly, then filling them with water and placing them next to thirsty plants (or you can invest in AquaSpikes, megagro.com/aquaspikes.htm, for a more scientific approach for repurposing plastic bottles). Also, just because a **garden hose** has sprung a leak, don't throw that away! Inexpensive hose couplings and repair kits not only allow you to salvage otherwise good garden hoses, but to cut and recouple them in configurations to make a customized irrigation (slow drip or full blast) specifically for your garden.

And for watering bigger areas and larger plants, fill the empty **plastic bladder** from a five-liter box of wine with water, then place it on its side with the spigot slightly open to produce the desired drip rate. This works particularly well for keeping newly transplanted trees and shrubs from dying of thirst . . . and of course the process of making a box-wine irrigation system ensures that the gardener won't die of thirst either.

## One-of-a-Kind Garden Art

Remember, *beauty is in the eye of the beholder* (including cheapskates), and when it comes to garden art, anything goes. I've seen beautiful mosaic stepping-stones and garden wall hangings made out of **broken porcelain china** embedded safely in cement, colorful hummingbird feeders and pinwheels fashioned from **plastic soda bottles**, attractive planters made from old **car tires** (painted to look like terra-cotta or a rainbow of other colors), and a fascinating garden mobile made from recycled **bicycle wheels**. It's all about just getting creative with what you have.

**Hubcaps** are also a favorite medium among garden-variety repurposing artists. Whether simply hung on a garden wall, transformed into a revolving mobile, or turned skyward to serve as a chrome-plated birdbath, hubcaps really are works of art in their own right when you stop and look at them.

Pennsylvania artist Ken Marquis has become so enamored with hubcaps as "metal canvases," he's founded Landfillart (landfillart.org), which he defines as "an international effort encompassing 1,041 artists to claim a piece of rusted metal garbage and create fine art." In this case, the "rusted metal garbage" Ken is referring to is hubcaps, lots and lots of hubcaps. He ships old hubcaps to artists all around the world who have agreed to do their thing using the round metal canvas he provides as part of what Ken envisions as the largest collaborative arts project in history (that's human history, not just the history of hubcap art). Eventually Ken plans to launch a traveling exhibit featuring two hundred of the most representative metal canvases. Check out the truly fine art being created through the Landfillart project, and I'll bet that next time you see an orphaned hubcap by the side of the road, you'll pull over and pick it up.

## More Nifty-Thrifty Repurposing Tips for the Garden and Yard

- Use screws to fasten a heavy-gauge **plastic nursery pot** to an outside wall or inside the garage; it makes a handy spool to coil extension cords and light garden hoses around when they're not in use.

- If you have a fish pond or other water garden, once again old **pantyhose** come in handy. Fill a length of pantyhose with gravel and soil, tie it off, and plant water lilies and other aquatic plants in it on the bottom of the pond. Cut a small opening for the plants to grow through.

- Keep cut flowers from the garden fresher by putting a couple of pieces of leftover **charcoal** in the bottom of a flower vase after you pick them. It will keep the water clean and clear, and the flowers last longer.

- To keep pots and other planting containers from getting so heavy that you can't move them, fill the base with a layer of **foam** packing **"peanuts,"** then cover with potting soil. Not only do they lighten the load, but they provide good drainage for container plants both inside and outside the home.

- And, of course, what's a garden without plants? Rather than throw away the **seeds** from vegetables and fruits, many types can be saved and used to grow a new round of crops next gardening season. Harvesting and storing seeds—and knowing which varieties work best—is a little complicated, but an article from the University of Minnesota Extension, at extension.umn.edu/garden/yard-garden/vegetables/harvesting-and-storing-home-garden-vegetables, explains it simply and well.

### The Landfill in My Backyard

People file NIMBY (Not in My Back Yard) lawsuits all the time when a county or other municipality wants to put a public landfill in their neighborhood. In my case, I nearly had to take my long-suffering wife to court in order to convince her to *let me* put a landfill in our backyard.

You'd never know it, but when you kick back in one of the comfy Adirondack chairs on a shady little hillside terrace in our backyard, you're actually sitting on a **toilet** . . . or maybe in a **bathtub** or **sink**.

The pretty garden spot didn't exist before I remodeled one of our bathrooms and used the plumbing fixtures and other nonhazardous construction rubble (including broken-up **ceramic tile**, **drywall**, and **scrap lumber**) to backfill the new terrace area I'd secured to the hillside with a retaining wall built from pressure-treated landscape timbers. I compacted the debris and then covered it with a good foot of fill dirt and topsoil, which is now covered with a small swath of lush lawn surrounded by ferns and hostas.

And that was just the start of our backyard landfill. I added dozens of **glass bottles** and pieces of **broken glass** to the concrete slab I poured for our backyard patio (of course, the broken chards of glass were safely entombed within the concrete, with flagstones set in mortar placed over the top). That was a real win-win project, since it was so hot while I was mixing and pouring the concrete, I managed to stretch the concrete mix significantly by adding the bottles from all the beer I was downing as I worked. (I wonder why that patio is a little lopsided?)

Then there's the interesting little grassy knoll at the edge of our property that helps to provide some privacy and reduce the noise of passing traffic. Buried safely underneath it is an **old stove**, a couple of **automobile rims**, and some broken-up **chunks of concrete** our neighbor gave me in exchange for helping him tear up his old driveway.

If you have the space, why not give nonhazardous household items like these a safe and proper burial in your own backyard, rather than ship them off to one of America's two thousand overflowing landfills? Most of the stuff ends up in the ground either way, but at least in your backyard you can create some interesting landscaping features with them, like our "commodious" toilet garden.

# Chapter 8
## A Salute to Composting and Specialized Recycling

**Answer:** *I put an old* **brick** *or* **phone book** *in a* **cardboard box** *and tape the postcard or envelope to the front, as a mailing label. Then I mail the box back to them, with a note inside asking them to please remove my name from their mailing list. Since they have to pay for return postage by the ounce, it costs them a fortune and you'll never hear from them again.*
William U. (Denver, Colorado)

**Question:** *What do you do with return* **"postage-paid" reply cards and envelopes** *you get in* **junk mail***?* (Well, that's one way to get taken off unwanted mailing lists! See officeofstrategicinfluence.com/bulkmailer/)

I want to believe that there's a special place in heaven for creative repurposers and anybody who makes it a point to live a little lighter on the planet before they ascend to that great recycling bin in the sky. I'm sure if there is such a place, you'll be surrounded by all the trees and other natural resources you helped to save while on earth, rather than haunted by everything you wasted or unnecessarily destroyed.

And if that's what heaven is like, composters and other people who really go the extra-extra mile to thoughtfully dispose of things they no longer need will no doubt be among the most venerated of all heavenly residents. Regardless of your religious beliefs (or lack thereof), wastefulness is universally considered wrong:

- In the Bible, Proverbs 18:9 reads, "He also that is slothful in his work is brother to him that is a great waster."

- Buddhists use the term *mottainai* to express regret and condemnation when something useful is wasted, misused, or disrespected.

- The Quran warns: "Eat of the good things. We have provided for your sustenance, but commit no excess therein, lest My Wrath should descend on you."

- Judaism teaches *bal tashchit*, the principle that it is wrong to waste or unnecessarily destroy anything of value.

- For Hindus, "protection and reverence for the Earth" is one of the modes of Sattva, the key virtues that devotees are instructed to follow for a purposeful life.

- Or, if you're like me and you're more of a follower of the Church of Will Rogers, here's what our spiritual leader had to say: "Too

many people spend money they haven't
earned, to buy things they don't want, to im-
press people they don't like."

No matter how you say it, waste is bad. Amen.

## Composting: A Rind Is a Terrible Thing to Waste

Composting—turning unwanted organic material into
humus, a superrich soil additive for the garden—is in
many ways the ultimate act of frugality. You're not
only saving money by making use of would-be organic throwaways, but you're keeping them out of the
landfill.

If you've priced commercially-produced compost at
the garden center, you know why it's sometimes called
"the black gold of the garden." Composting is easy and
even kind of fun. Everyone can join in the rot-fest,
even urban pioneers; if done properly, compost is odor-
less and of little interest to pests. Here's how:

**Build or Buy a Compost Bin:** Square, round, rectan-
gular, triangular, or shaped like your girlfriend's butt,
your bin should be roughly equal in height, width, and
depth (typically three or four feet). You can make one
by simply forming wire fencing into a cylinder or other
free-form shape, or use lumber to construct a sturdier
bin (although it's hard to build a butt shape out of lumber). I built my compost bin—a.k.a. "Gomer the Pile"
(get it?)—from leftover **lumber** from a deck-build-
ing project. Now that's repurposing times two! Urban

gardeners should consider buying a compact plastic "rolling" compost bin from the garden center. Those keep the compost up off the ground and can be used on decks or patios. If possible, place your bin in a shady location.

**Add Brown and Green:** I like to think of composting as making "soil lasagna," since—just like when making lasagna—layering is the secret to a successful recipe. Rotate layers of brown material, like dried **leaves, twigs, straw, pine needles,** and **wood chips,** with thinner layers of green organic materials like **grass clippings** and **leaves, fruit and vegetable trimmings,** and **weeds.** Never compost meat products, pet/human feces, diseased plant materials, or those treated with herbicides or that have already gone to seed. Water each layer thoroughly as you go.

**Stir, Cover and Let Cook:** After a week or two, mix together the layers using a pitchfork or other tool. Then cover with a tarp to retain moisture and heat. That way it'll really start to cook, fast-tracking the decomposition process. Sit back and let nature do the work. Your compost should be handsomely decayed and ready to use in just two or three months, depending on conditions. In general, the larger the volume of the pile, the faster it decays. Keeping it moist by occasionally adding water will also expedite the process. Compost is ready to use when the source material is thoroughly decayed—looking more like soil than its original ingredients—with particles of different decomposed materials broken down to the point where their source is all but indistinguishable.

Once your compost pile is up-and-rotting, always ask yourself one simple question before you throw something in the trash: *Gee, I wonder if I can compost that instead?* You might be surprised by some of the answers. Consider these curious composting commodities:

- **Beer and wine**—Gomer likes a stale brewski every once in a while. The dregs from home brewing and wine making can also be composted.
- **Bread and other grain products**—including **pasta**, **rice**, **cereal**, **crackers**, **pizza crusts**, and so on, but bury them in the pile to deter unwanted pests.
- **Bouquets** and **houseplants** that have bitten the dust.
- **Clothing/fabric** made from natural fibers (e.g., cotton, wool, silk, etc.).
- **Coffee grounds** and **paper coffee filters.**
- **Cotton balls** and **cotton Q-tips** with cardboard or wooden sticks (NOT plastic).
- **Corks** and **cork products.**
- **Dryer lint.**
- **Eggshells** and **whole eggs** that are past their prime.
- Evergreen **Christmas wreaths**, **roping**, and **trees** (chop or shred bigger branches).

- **Fireplace ashes**.
- **Hair** and **fur** (your own and your pets').
- **Jell-O (gelatin)**—Gomer says: "There's always room for Jell-O."
- **Leather goods** and **leather clothing**, like your leftover lederhosen.
- **Masking tape**.
- **Milk** and other **spoiled dairy products**.
- **Nail clippings** (human and pet, unpolished).
- **Pet food leftovers**: Dry pet food is okay for the compost pile, but bury it in the pile to deter rodents and other unwanted pests.
- **Rope** and **string** made from natural fibers (e.g., cotton, hemp, jute, etc.).
- **Sawdust**.
- **Seaweed** and **kelp**.
- **Teabags** and **loose tea**.
- **Urine**.
- **Vacuum cleaner bags (paper)** and its **non-synthetic contents**.
- **White glue**—check for toxic ingredients, but most white glues like Elmer's brand are fine.
- And last but not least, **latex condoms** and cotton/cardboard **feminine hygiene products**—Yes, it's true. Yes, it's gross.

### Shocking Eco Facts

If plastic garbage bags can take up to five hundred years to decompose in a landfill, you're probably wondering about the "rot rate" of other things we throw away. Here's some figures compiled by the University of

Utah: * **Aluminum** takes 200–500 years to degrade in a landfill; recycling aluminum takes 95 percent less energy than making aluminum from raw materials. * **Glass** takes 1,000,000 years to fully degrade; recycling glass takes only 30 percent of the energy required to manufacture new glass. * **Plastic bottles** can take 1,000 years to degrade; recycling plastic bottles uses 88 percent less energy than making plastic from raw materials. Even so, because of other environmental and health impacts associated with plastics, using aluminum or glass containers is always preferable. * Uncoated **paper** products typically decompose within just a year or two, but recycling paper uses 60 percent less energy—and generates 74 percent less air pollution—than manufacturing new paper. * **Steel** takes up to 100 years to fully degrade. Even though recycling steel takes 25 percent less energy and generates 75 percent less water and air pollution than making new, we still throw away 70 percent of all the metal we use. That's enough to supply all U.S. auto manufacturers with 100 percent of the steel and iron they use every year.

## Finding a Special Home for Your Special Things

Like a lot of people, I fight a constant battle to control clutter around the house. It's a battle I often lose. A year ago I vowed to undertake a major decluttering campaign to rid my life and our house of things I no longer use. The problem was, that resolution got stuck in line behind my earlier resolution, the one about overcoming my tendency to procrastinate. So, you know what happened.

When I finally sat down and confronted my Inner Slob—surrounded by piles of stuff I just couldn't seem to let go of—it hit me: *Man, I've got some really cool stuff!* I mean, unlike your stuff, my stuff is *really* special. I can't throw it away, and I can't sell it or give it to just anyone. *My stuff* is way too special for that.

That's when I started to do some research into organizations that could help me pass along my precious possessions to someone who will truly appreciate and use them. Of course, thrift stores operated by charities like Salvation Army (salvationarmyusa.org), Goodwill (goodwill.org), and other local groups deserve our support and donated items, too. But if, like me, you have a few things that are so very near and dear to you, here are some special ways to part with them.

**Bicycles:** Since I'm a bicycle fanatic, I have more than a few spare ones out in the garage. In fact, over the course of forty years of cycling, during my daily rides I've actually *found* half a dozen perfectly good bikes abandoned alongside the road! Of course sometimes I like to use old **bicycles** and their parts as works of art around the house (see Chapter 2), but how many Picasso Pedal Pushers does one really have room to properly display? So I'm going to donate some of my old friends to Bikes for the World (bikesfortheworld.org), a nonprofit organization that provides used bicycles to people in Third

World countries who rely on bikes for daily transportation, not just recreation.

**Business Clothing:** Thankfully, I no longer need to wear a suit and tie every day, so I'm only hanging on to a couple of suits in the collection of business attire I amassed during the years I spent working in "real jobs." The others I plan to donate to Career Gear (careergear. org), a nonprofit organization that distributes business **clothing** to disadvantaged men who are trying to re-enter the workforce. Dress for Success (dressforsuccess. org) is a similar nonprofit organization that accepts donations of professional attire for needy women.

**Children's Books:** My duplicate copy of *Stuart Little*, one of my all-time favorite **books**, will find a good home and delight some young reader when I donate it to Project Night Night (projectnighnight.org), a nonprofit organization that provides "Night Night" tote bags filled with books and other items to homeless children.

**Eyeglasses:** For someone who has never worn prescription **eyeglasses**, I don't know why or how I've amassed so many pairs of them, let alone why I insist on hanging on to them. Do I really think that this pair of glasses that I found—like so many things—in a ditch while bicycling down some godforsaken highway will someday be exactly the pair of prescription glasses I'll require when my vision loss finally catches up with my hair loss? Instead, I'm going to donate them to the life-changing eyeglass recycling program sponsored by Lions Clubs International (lionsclubs.org/EN/our-work/sight-programs/eyeglass-recycling/).

**Musical Instruments:** I feel good about donating the used saxophone I bought during my short-lived Kenny G. phase to the Mr. Holland's Opus Foundation (mhopus.org), a nonprofit organization that refurbishes used **musical instruments** and gives them to underfunded school musical programs. (Plus, I admit it, I cry like a kid on the first day of kindergarten every time I watch that organization's movie namesake.)

**Running Shoes:** Sadly, the pair I bought five years ago is almost as good as new . . . another resolution that bit the dust. There are many charitable organizations that provide used athletic **shoes** to those less fortunate, and worn-out shoes can also be recycled into building materials. Check out the website recycledrunners.com for shoe recycling facilities and nonprofit organizations near you.

**Sports Equipment:** I've decided to donate the speed bag that nearly knocked *me* out last time I tried to use it to SportsGift.org, so that they can pass it along to an aspiring Muhammad Ali. After all, I always know that I can make another speed bag from a worn-out **football** (see Chapter 5) if I ever decide to make a comeback. Sports Gift is a nonprofit organization that uses donated **sports equipment** to create community-based sports programs for underprivileged kids around the world.

**Unused Gift Cards:** According to a study by the Tower-Group, every year roughly $5 billion in value is lost on unused **gift cards**. I found four partially used gift cards during my de-cluttering campaign, each with such a small credit balance that I knew I'd end up spending more on stuff I really don't need if I went shopping to redeem them. Instead, I donated the balances to charities through websites like GiftCardGiver.com.

**Old Magazines**: And finally, I think I'll take my big stack of old **magazines**—including *Saxophone Monthly, Runner's World,* and *Boxing Digest*—over to the local hospital and some area retirement homes to see if they would like some reading material.

Knowing that my special stuff found some very special new homes really got me motivated to make good on my decluttering resolution. Now, I wonder if there's a charity worthy of my Chia Pet collection?

## More Nifty-Thrifty Tips for Composting and Specialized Recycling

While there are plenty of ways to repurpose all these items, here are some ways to get rid of them without—dare I even say it?—throwing them away.

**Blankets, Towels, and Linens:** Local animal shelters often need donations of such items to use in animal cages. Visit animalshelter.org to find animal shelters near you.

**Phone Books:** Over half a billion phone books (white and yellow pages) are printed each year . . . that's about nineteen million trees worth. Not all curbside recycling programs accept phone books. You can go to earth911. com to find a phone book recycling center near you or—if you don't want to receive phone books in the first place—go to one of these websites to opt out: yellowpagesgoesgreen.org, yellowpagesoptout.com.

**Foam Peanuts and Bubble Wrap:** Some municipal recyclers accept them, but a number of shipping services are glad to reuse them if you just drop them off. You can find a nationwide directory of packaging material recyclers at packingrecyclers.com or contact local branches of UPS Stores (theupsstore.com) or Mail Boxes Etc. (mbe.com) to see if they're interested.

**Plastic Nursery Pots:** They can usually be recycled at the curbside or, better yet, sometimes returned to the nursery for a small credit. Check with your nursery or recycling center.

**Cell Phones:** Caution should be taken when disposing of unwanted cell phones, since they contain toxic metals that are harmful to the environment. This nonprofit organization can help you safely recycle them: recyclemycellphone.org. But you may want to hang on to your old cell phones, since under federal law they must be capable of dialing 911 in case of an emergency, even if the service contract has expired (obviously the phone must still be in working condition). Why not stash your old cell phones around the house, car, and so on just in case?

**Books:** Many public libraries accept donations of used books, which they normally resell to raise operating funds. You can also recycle old books by swapping them for some new reads on websites like PaperBack-Swap.com, BookMooch.com, and titletrader.com.

**Junk Mail:** While taping a postage-paid reply card to a brick and sending it back to a bothersome junk mailer at their expense will mostly get your name taken off their list pronto, there's an easier way to avoid getting unwanted junk mail. Nonprofit organizations like dmachoice.org and 41pounds.org can help you do it. By the way, "41 pounds" is the amount of junk mail the average American adult receives every year!

## They Recycle THAT?

Even though more than 80 percent of U.S. households have easy access to locally based programs for recycling paper, plastic, glass, and aluminum, sometimes there are items you'd like to recycle that fall outside those categories. Nonprofit organizations and specialized businesses are springing up everywhere to recycle almost everything imaginable. Here are some of the more unusual ones I've come across.

**Adult Novelties:** The creative reposers at Sex Toy Recycling (sextoyrecycling.com/) are in the business of doing just as their name implies, so be forewarned before you go to their website. Didn't their mothers ever warn them about playing with things when you don't know where they've been?

**Hotel Soap Slivers:** As we've seen in other chapters, those little slivers of soap can be repurposed in plenty of ways—from making a cheapskate-soap-on-a-rope to cooking a dirty snowball to deterring deer. Now many hotel chains are recycling their leftover soap and shampoo either in-house or by joining forces with nonprofit organizations like Clean the World (cleantheworld.org) to recycle it and donate it to those in need.

**Dentures:** *There's gold in that there mouth!* Most dentures contain about $50 worth of precious metals, including silver and gold, and the world chews through about 3.6 million sets every year. Surprisingly, most unwanted dentures are thrown away. But a nonprofit organization in Japan (ireba-recycle.com/index.html) recycles the metals found in dentures and donates the funds to UNICEF. So far they've raised more than $250,000, and they're looking for charitable-minded colleagues around the world who would like to replicate their program. Now that's a fund-raising project you can sink your teeth into.

**Bras:** The Bra Recyclers (brarecycling.com) helps to collect and redistribute used and unused bras to deserving women in developing countries and in the

United States as they transition back to self-sufficiency. As the company's website says, they do this through a "support network [*apparently no pun intended*] of Bra Recycling Ambassadors." A directory of local drop-off locations is available on the website, as well as instructions for mailing unwanted bras to a centralized collection facility in Arizona.

**Human Hair:** Nowadays even smaller quantities of human hair—including much of what used to end up in the wastebasket at the beauty parlor—is now being recycled and used for everything from deer-repellent garden products to cleaning up oil spills. And unless you're hair-follicle-challenged like me, consider donating your hair to Locks of Love (locksoflove.org), a nonprofit organization that recycles healthy human hair into hairpieces for financially disadvantaged children suffering from medical hair loss.

**Prosthetic Limbs:** According to the website of the Amputee Coalition of America (amputee-coalition. org/fact_sheets/pros_limb_donations.html), "Prosthetic components are generally not reused in the United States because of legal considerations. However, used prosthetic limbs may be disassembled and the components shipped to Third World countries for use by landmine victims and/or other individuals in need." Their website includes a list of organizations in the United States that accept donations of prosthetics.

**Diapers:** With cloth diapers nearly a thing of the past, disposing of so-called disposable diapers is easier said than done. Consider that the average baby requires about six thousand disposable diapers prior to potty training—no wonder our landfills runneth over. But a British company cleverly named Knowaste (Knowaste. com) is pioneering a system for recycling disposable diapers, or disposable "nappies" as the sophisticated Brits call them.

**Mattresses:** Old mattresses are difficult to give away or even throw away. Did you know that many mattress retailers now accept used mattresses for recycling? That's good news for the environment, because about 90 percent of an old mattress can be recycled into fiber for clothing, wood chips, foam products, and scrap metal. Check with your local mattress sellers to see if they offer recycling. I'll sleep better tonight knowing that my old mattress didn't end up in a landfill, like so many of the twenty million mattresses we replace every year in the United States.

**Coffins:** And speaking of sleep, recycled coffins? Caskets can now be rented at many funeral homes rather than purchasing one if you're planning on being cremated . . . or think you might still snap out of it. Also, for regular burial or cremation, cardboard coffins—many of which are made from 100 percent recycled materials—are often the least expensive and most eco-friendly way to "go." Truly a diehard creative repurposer until the very end. (greatgreengoods. com/2005/08/08/environmentally-friendlycasket/).

# Final Round of Repurposing Madness: The 35 Missing Tips

**Answer:** *It's not as good as the real thing, but I can tell ya it'll work in a pinch. The trick is finding one with the right cup size . . . especially if it ain't your wife's.*
Joe B. (Uniontown, Pennsylvania)

**Question:** *What can you do with a worn-out **bra**?*
(Joe B., a carpenter, is talking about repurposing a single cup and part of the strap from an old bra to use as a dust mask when he finds himself without a standard mask on the job site. One might wonder why he'd have an old bra with him instead, but that's another question.)

After adding together all the repurposing tips found in the preceding chapters, I discovered that I was short exactly 35 tips to bring the TTC ("Total

Tip Count") to 1,001, as promised on the cover of this book.

I may be cheap—in fact I consider that a virtue—but I'm also honest. I always want to give you your money's worth. So here are the 35 Missing Tips.

1. The **plastic bladder** from an empty five-liter box of wine makes a perfect inflatable travel pillow. And trust me, when you get on an airplane and start inflating it, the guy next to you will immediately move to another seat and leave you extra room to stretch out. What a bonus!

2. If you've lost a **mitten**—or have a **glove** or even a **sock** without a mate—tether it to your ice scraper with a piece of string and keep it in the glove compartment of your car. Your scraping hand will thank you for it some icy morning.

3. Cut the cuffs off old long-sleeved **shirts and sweaters**, and use them as conversation-starting sleeves to slip over hot cups of coffee.

4. Old **sweaters** (torso portion, front and/or back) make distinctive and durable cushion covers to replace worn-out upholstery on straight-backed chairs.

5. **Newspapers** can be made into "logs" for the fireplace. Start with a **cardboard paper towel tube** and begin wrapping individual unfolded sections (no more than ten pages at a time) as tightly as possible around the tube. Lightly

spray paper log with water between each section, until the log is four to six inches in diameter. Secure with string and allow it to dry for a couple of weeks before burning.

6. Save your **dryer lint** and stuff it into **cardboard toilet paper and paper towel tubes** to use in starting fires in the fireplace or woodstove. Dryer lint is highly flammable, so these little "TP Logs," as I call them, make fire starting easy.

7. **Toilet paper tubes** are an easy way to keep small extension cords neat and handy; just coil the cord and insert it through the tube.

8. Glue old **corks** in a simple frame and use as either a trivet on the table or hang it on the wall as a genuine "cork board."

9. Use **banana peels** to shine the leaves on your houseplants—it'll make them sparkle and acts as a natural pesticide and fertilizer too.

10. Put **foam packing peanuts** in a **plastic bag** and stuff it in your ice chest to fill any voids. The added insulation will help keep the contents cool for longer.

11. A spare or worn-out **boot or shoe** makes a cute planter or vase for a flower arrangement; line with a **plastic bag** or cut a **plastic soda bottle** to fit inside to hold the soil/water.

12. Carry an old **CD** or **DVD** in your emergency kit to use as you would a mirror in signaling for help or rescue.

13. **Plastic soda straws** can be squished flat, cut in half, and then woven together to make interesting and durable cocktail coasters. Cut a square of felt to fit underneath, and then secure with glue or stitch a seam around the edge to keep the weave from unraveling.

14. Not recommended, but apparently true: According to a 2007 article on the website News.Com.au, used **condoms** were being recycled into hair bands in southern China and were selling quite well until some crazy physicians raised potential health concerns. (Go figure.)

15. Although not really a way to repurpose *used* **condoms**, if you have a new one left over (maybe you were a bit too optimistic last time you went to the drugstore?), it's a good place to keep an emergency supply of matches dry during wilderness outings. Put the matches inside a nonlubricated condom and tie it off. See, you *knew* you'd eventually have a chance to use it.

16. Under the category "Gross, But Maybe Not by Southern China Standards": A number of my Miser Advisers report that they hang on to their used **Q-tips** to use in detailing their cars (inside and out) and cleaning hard-to-reach spaces on their fine wood furniture. According to them, a little earwax beats commercial products like Turtle Wax and Lemon Pledge hands down.

17. A single old **bicycle inner tube** can be cut crossways with scissors to make about a billion rubber bands. They also make great "bungee-style" cords for strapping stuff down when you attach a couple of "S" hooks sold at any hardware store.

18. Miser Adviser Fred T. likes to use his old **bicycle inner tubes** to construct a giant water balloon slingshot between two trees. Watch out for that guy.

19. Hollow out an old **book** or even a **phone book** using a utility knife and straightedge to make a "book safe" to hide your valuables in.

20. Another place to hide jewelry and other valuables—perhaps even safer than Grandma Yeager's freezer—is inside an empty **deodorant container** (stick type) or inside an empty **toothpaste tube** (slit open the end). These tips are particularly useful when traveling.

21. **Toothpaste tubes** can also be cut open at the end, washed out, and refilled with grease to use as a handy grease gun, or with peanut butter or other foods for your next backpacking trip. Reseal the cut-open end with a binder clip.

22. Used **fabric softener sheets** make great general household wipes for dusting, cleaning windows, and so on. They can even be used in place of the wipes sold for popular Swiffer Sweeper mops.

23. I also like to put a used **fabric softener sheet** between every couple of books on my bookshelves or between books I have in cold storage. It helps to keep them from getting that musty smell and mildewing.

24. Put an empty **plastic soda bottle** in an **old sock** (or one missing its mate), tie it off, and it makes a terrific dog or cat toy. Pets love the crunching noise it makes when they play with it.

25. Add a couple of pieces of **charcoal** left over from the summer grilling season to the bags of rock salt and sand you stockpile in the garage in preparation for the winter storms; it absorbs moisture and keeps salt and sand from caking up.

26. An empty cardboard **tissue box**—or a **coffee can** with a slot cut in the plastic top—makes a convenient way to store and dispense your stockpile of **plastic shopping bags**.

27. Old **tennis balls** are really handy for marking and padding potentially dangerous objects like metal posts and stakes sticking out of the ground. Just cut a small incision in the ball and stick it on.

28. A flattened **aluminum can**—fastened on with pipe clamps—is a temporary fix for holes in a rusted muffler. At least it will silence it enough to keep the cops off your tailpipe.

29. As automotive urban legend has it, a length of **pantyhose** really can be substituted for a broken fan belt in a pinch, provided that it's a short trip to the repair shop and she isn't fond of ultrasheer hose.

30. And the last pantyhose tip in this book—I promise! Photo buffs, try stretching a length of old **pantyhose** over your camera lens for a cool muted or starburst effect. (Note: It's best to have her take them off before you try this.)

31. **Baby food jars** and **pill bottles** are of course perfect for storing all types of tiny, easily lost items . . . buttons, nuts and bolts, spare change, and the teeth you lost as a kid that the Tooth Fairy never did come to get out of hock. But get even more organized in the workshop or sewing room by screwing the lids of the bottles to all four sides of a twelve-inch piece of **scrap lumber** (4x4 is perfect), then mounting it on the wall—like a roll of paper towels—to use as a rotating caddy.

32. Make colorful "paper beads" by cutting glossy old **magazines** and **junk mail** into strips, coating the strips with glue or paste, then rolling them around a straight pin or piece of wire. When they dry, remove the pin/wire and re-string them to make jewelry or beaded curtains.

33. Do you brownbag your lunch? If so, you'll find that the heavy-duty, multilayered **paper bag** that five pounds of sugar typically comes

packaged in can be used and reused—day after day, month after month—for that purpose. One of my Miser Advisers has been packing his lunch in the same Domino's Sugar bag every workday for more than a year, and still counting. It's his "cheapskate sack of pride," and it's pretty stylin'.

34. Another good alternative to traditional, disposable lunch bags are the wax-coated **air sickness bags** that you find in the proverbial "seat pocket in front of you" whenever you fly. They're a little small—but perfect for carrying a single sandwich—and they last forever.

35. And finally, while on the subject of **air sickness bags**, they also work really well as luminaries. Cut a heart shape or your lover's initials in both sides of the bag to release more light, and put a little sand and an LED "fake" candle in the bottom.

Nothing says *con amore* like an air sickness bag luminary on the dinner table. Call me a hopeless romantic . . . or maybe just hopeless.

And then there were 1,001.

Thanks for taking the time to read this book. I hope you've enjoyed our little romp through the wild, wonderful, sometimes wacky world of creative repurposing.

Hopefully you've learned some new ways to reuse stuff that might otherwise end up in the trash. Even more important, I hope this book has helped you gain a new appreciation for how something as simple as re-using a plastic bag can help you save both money and planet Earth.

And I just want you to know that next time you're headed toward the trash can, I'll be watching. Reduce, **reuse**, recycle . . . but whatever you do, *Don't Throw That Away!*

Keep in touch and send me your tips for creative re-purposing via my website (UltimateCheapskate.com) or e-mail me at UltCheapskate@aol.com.

Stay Cheap!
– Jeff Yeager, The Ultimate Cheapskate

# INDEX BY ITEM

*Don't Throw That Away!*

**Fruit and vegetable trimmings:**

# Acknowledgments

Those of us who research or practice within the Sciences of Creative Repurposing know that it would be sheer hubris to claim credit for any specific repurposing method or concept. As with any science, we are simply expanding the body of knowledge that is already out there, building upon it one foam packing peanut or turkey giblet at a time.

So this book truly represents a collaborative effort, and I have many people to thank for making it possible:

- First and foremost, I must thank my world-wide network of Miser Advisers for so many of the innovative tips and tricks contained in this book—you're the best, even though I'll always be the cheapest.

- Of course there would be no book if there was no publisher. Thank you Random House/Three Rivers Press for first publishing this book, and thank you Stacey Glick and Sharon Pelletier of Dystel & Goderich Literary Management for helping me release this self-published version. I owe a Costco-sized debt of gratitude to my able assistant Adam Lucas for all of his hard work in making this new edition even better than the original.

- Denise, my long-suffering wife, worked tirelessly on the research and photography that went into this book (and kindly looked the other way whenever I commandeered the kitchen for "a few little repurposing experiments"), and I love her all the more because of it.

And finally, as you know from the preceding pages, I owe a tremendous debt of gratitude to Allen Gant, the inventor of pantyhose, without which the Sciences of Creative Repurposing would be like a screen door with a gaping hole in it. (Although, by the way, you can easily repair that with a worn-out pair of pantyhose.)

# About the Author

Jeff Yeager spent twenty-four years managing national nonprofit organizations before launching his current career as a writer, public speaker, and media personality in 2004. His previous books include *The Ultimate Cheapskate's Road Map to True Riches*, *The Cheapskate Next Door*, and *How to Retire the Cheapskate Way*, all published by Random House imprints. He is AARP's official Savings Expert and host of *The Cheap Life with Jeff Yeager*, a weekly web show on YouTube produced by AARP (www.YouTube.com/CheapLifeChannel). Jeff lives happily and frugally in Accokeek, Maryland, with his pooooor wife, Denise, and his beloved compost pile, Gomer. Contact Jeff via his website (www.UlimateCheapskate.com) and follow him on Twitter (@JeffYeager) and Facebook (www.facebook.com/JeffYeagerUltimateCheapskate).

Made in the USA
Lexington, KY
21 July 2015